D0923003

Che questo sacrificio serva per il rispetto
della religione e della razza ... !!

We must not forget Anne's sweet smile...
It will lead us to a better world
We have to really understand her..

Ramy Papadopoulos

Anne Frank é a vítima de uma triste guerra.
Em tôdas as partes do mundo outras pequenas Annes
sofrem o terror da guerra...
A mensagem que Ela deu ao mundo é linda e
aqui podemos concretizar o quadro que seu diá-
rio retrata tão bem.

São Paulo — BRASIL

25. 8. 1968

We say more about peace and harmony among people
irrespective of creed, colour or race. But do we really
believe and do what we say?

Bediako Asare
GHANA — WEST AFRICA

an unforgettable visit to this house
where Anne Frank and her family
lived in hiding. after having read
her diary several times, I was so
glad I was finally able to see this house
She was a wonderful girl,
Kristiansand,
Oslo, Norway

A Tribute to Anne Frank

A Tribute to Anne Frank

Edited by Anna G. Steenmeijer

In collaboration with

Otto Frank
Henri van Praag, chairman of the Anne Frank Foundation

Doubleday & Company, Inc.
Garden City, New York
1971

This book has been initiated, arranged and produced by
Frank Fehmers Productions, Amsterdam, Holland.

Layout and design by Marc de Klijn.

Printed and bound by Van Leer, Proost en Brandt, Amsterdam, Holland.

Library of Congress Catalog Card Number 70-130885

Translation copyright © 1970 by Doubleday & Company, Inc.
Copyright © 1970 by Otto Frank

All Rights Reserved

Printed in Holland
First Edition in the United States of America

Contents

I see the world gradually being turned into a wilderness, I hear the ever approaching thunder, which will destroy us too, I can feel the sufferings of millions and yet, if I look up into the heavens, I think that it will all come right, that this cruelty too will end, and that peace and tranquillity will return again. **Diary - July 15, 1944**

Dedication

The letters I have received over the years from readers of the diary are evidence of the tremendous influence it has had on people of many nationalities, especially on young people. For that reason, I have often been asked to authorize their publication.

While aware of the great psychological and educational value of such a collection, I found the content of many letters too personal to allow their publication. Then, when an anthology of the reactions to *The Diary of Anne Frank* was proposed, of which the letters would be a relatively small part, I agreed to give it my support, provided that the writers of the letters consented to their publication.

I believe it will be interesting and valuable to many people to see how great the influence of this diary has been, a diary written by a young girl during those years when she and her family had to hide from Nazi persecution because they were Jewish.

The many letters from young people indicate that they identify themselves with Anne, that her optimism and faith helps them to deal with their own problems. Many, inspired by her writings, reflect on the persecution of the Jews during the Hitler regime and make comparisons with the state of the world today. They see a world in which there are still wars, where people are still being persecuted and discriminated against for their faith, race, or convictions. Parents and teachers write that, after reading the diary and discussing it, they better understand their children and pupils and feel closer to them.

What has surprised me again and again, and still surprises me, is that the book as well as the play and the film based on it are not only known in Western Europe and the United States, but also in the communist countries, in South America, and in the countries of Asia. For me this is proof that the diary speaks to the hearts of people everywhere.

The many reactions of artists, amateur and professional, famous and unknown, are further evidence of the value of the diary as a human document. Some of those reactions appear in this book, and countless others have been inspired by, and dedicated to, the memory of Anne.

However touching and sincere the expressions of sympathy I receive may be, I always reply that it is not enough to think of Anne with pity or admiration. Her diary should be a source of inspiration toward the realization of the ideals and hopes she expressed in it.

To work in the spirit of these ideals is also the aim of the Anne Frank Foundation, which is itself perhaps the most important response to the diary. A chapter of this book is devoted to the scope and work of this organization.

Preface

Henri van Praag
Chairman of the Anne Frank Foundation

The Chinese sage Lao-tse once said: "One can know the whole world without ever leaving his own home." Every man holds the universe within his mind. Inside the four walls of a room, his imagination can take him anywhere. The human mind transcends time and space, to live in worlds where man in his body can never go.

The medieval monks made a virtue of necessity. The insecurity of life in the cities and villages compelled them to retreat to cloisters, where they developed new lives of the spirit. And in cloisters everywhere the vow of seclusion was freely taken by monks who found in this situation a deeper spiritual understanding and a simpler, more rewarding life. Exceptional writings have come out of seclusion. "Imitation of Christ," by Thomas a Kempis, is one in which man is challenged to a life of real humanity. The Roman philosopher Boethius had written "The Consolation of Philosophy" in his prison cell a thousand years earlier.

Here lies the function of the historical example. In this sense the Jewish people have been an example to other peoples in their suffering and in their hope for a better world. In the same way Anne Frank, as a Jewish child who suffered under the German occupation and nevertheless remained hopeful, was an example to the younger generation after the war.
One of the astonishing facts of the Second World War, in which millions of innocent people lost their lives, is that a young Jewish girl, in the confines of her tiny Annex, dreamed of a new world in which justice and peace would prevail. The Annex was both a cloister where its inhabitants were safe from the world, and a prison which they couldn't leave. This extraordinary experience, coupled with her suffering as a Jew, led this gifted and sensitive young girl to wisdom and maturity far beyond her years. Out of this experience came *The Diary of Anne Frank,* a human document known and loved throughout the world.

Presented as a dialogue with Kitty (which is the name of a school friend whom she greatly admired), Anne gives constant evidence of her growing mental maturity. Ultimately she writes: *If we bear all this sorrow and suffering, and there are still Jews left when it is over, then Jews, instead of being doomed, will be held up as an example. Who knows, it might even be our religion from which the world and all peoples learn good, and for that reason, and that reason alone, do we suffer now.*

That was more than a quarter of a century ago, yet we still live in a world in which the Jewish people suffer because of their belief, the Negro is persecuted in our most enlightened societies, millions of children live in fear and hunger, misunderstanding and hatred between people prevail, and we suffer constantly from man's inhumanity to man.

To you, the reader, and to us at the Anne Frank Foundation falls the task of changing these terrible conditions and creating, at last, a world in which peace, brotherhood, and justice prevail, a world in which no future Anne Frank will suffer in hiding, hardly daring to dream of the freedom that is every man's due.

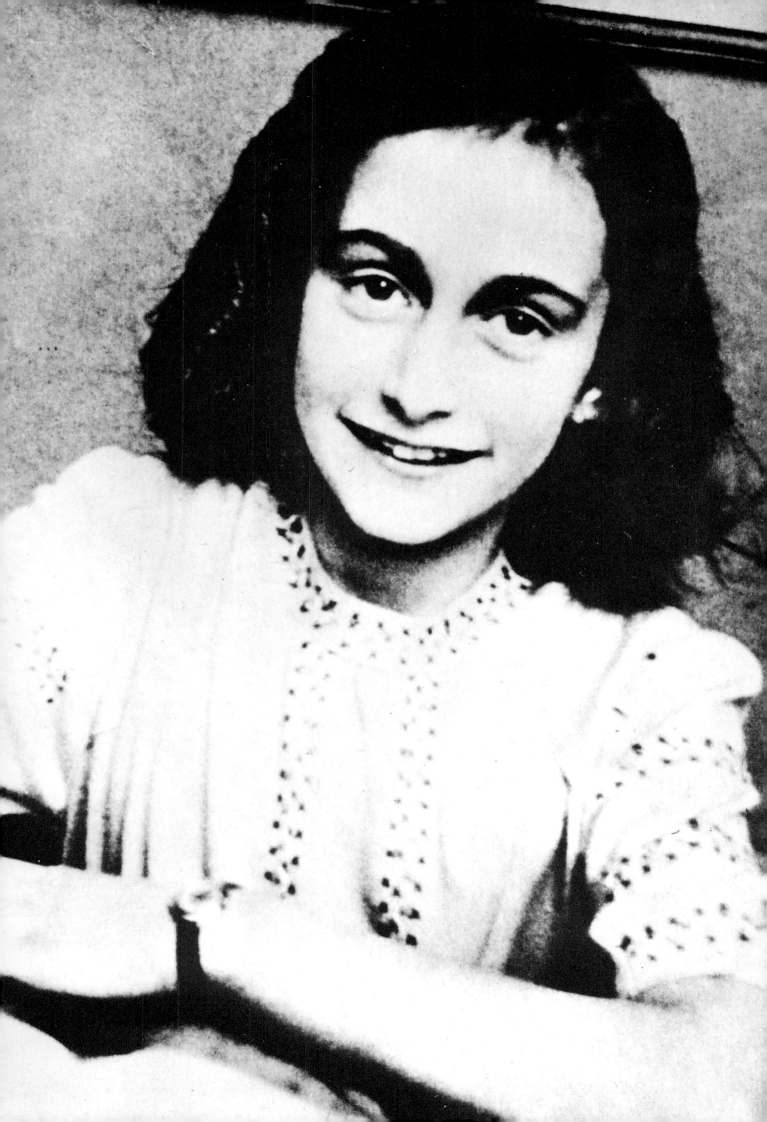

Hitler's Bid for Power

Marc de Klijn and Henri van Praag

In 1780 the German educator Salzmann wrote: *In the countries which we only visit in order to enrich ourselves with the native treasures, the degrading prejudice prevails that the original inhabitants of the country have no rights, and the Europeans have the unlimited right to mistreat them. This prejudice is breathed in by the European the moment that he sets foot on land, and he quickly feels the influence of that first breath on his heart. It would be easy for me to bring together numerous examples from every age and every region of similar insensibility to the suffering of one race in particular.*

There is no doubt that Salzmann was thinking of the Jews in this last passage. But in a more general way he wanted to criticize every sort of discrimination. And as a true educator he ended with a plea for the child, who is also often without rights.

In the history of National Socialism, too, the question arises of injustice towards other races and population groups, such as the Gypsies, the Jews, and millions of children.

Various historians have pointed out that the imperialistic oppression of the colored peoples was the model for Hitler's persecution of the Jews. While other countries such as England and France were able to build up world empires outside their own borders, it was extremely difficult for Germany to establish an external empire, partly because of the lack of sea power and, after the Treaty of Versailles (which Hitler always called a dictated agreement), the loss of those colonies which might have formed the nucleus of such an empire.

What happened then constituted a sort of internal imperialism. Jews and Gypsies were declared "non-German" (see the proclamation of the Berlin students, page 13) and thus attained the status of subject peoples. Thereafter, the government was free to confiscate their property, to abuse them, and to intern them in concentration camps.

As Machiavelli had advised earlier: *If your people are dissatisfied, pick out a group among them and treat it so badly that the others will find their lot endurable by comparison.*

Not by chance did the Jew become the scapegoat. The choice was linked to deeply rooted anti-Semitism in German society, which had religious, cultural, and economic bases.

In the nineteenth century there had been two official anti-Semitic parties in Germany, and the caricatures published in *Der Sturmer* had first appeared in the Middle Ages. Neither were pogroms invented by Adolf Hitler; throughout the late Middle Ages the Jews were persecuted throughout the Rhine area.

Sociologically, one could say that a feudal world was unable to tolerate Jewish "patterns of thought." Feudalism is static; Judaism is dynamic, looking forward to a new world. Hitler was the exponent of feudalism; he believed in the inequality of man, in masters and slaves, and he reinstituted in Germany the social ills of the Middle Ages.

One can partially explain the rise of Nazism by the particularly unfavorable economic circumstances in Germany after World War I, especially after the great inflation. One can also point to the humiliation for Germany in the occupation of the Rhine area by the allied troops. But the real reason lay much deeper, in the attempt to hold on to a philosophy of life which is impossible to maintain in the twentieth century.

The great mocker, Heinrich Heine, had already predicted the coming of Nazism a century before — with the swastika:

Christianity — and that is its greatest virtue — has somewhat softened the brute German militancy, but it could not destroy it completely, and if this taming talisman, the cross, is once broken, the wildness of the old warriors roars out again. . . the old stone gods rise up out of the ruins and rub the dust of a thousand years out of their eyes. . . The thunder in Germany is also German, and not very flexible; it is true that it comes rolling in very slowly, but it will come, and when you finally hear it crack it will be as if there had never been a crack of thunder before in the history of the world. Know then: the German thunder has finally reached its goal. . . a play will be staged in Germany, compared with which the French Revolution will seem like merely an innocent idyll.

And that play was staged.

1919
Founding of the DAP (Deutsche Arbeiter Partei: German Workers Party). Adolph Hitler is one of its core members. The founders aim to arouse a popular reactionary movement, especially against communism, and to stir up nationalism.

1920
Merging of the DAP and two other parties as the NSDAP (National Sozialistische Deutsche Arbeiter Partei: National Socialist German Workers Party). Drafting of the platform of the NSDAP. An extract from the official program demonstrates clearly the anti-Semitism of this party:

Art. 4: A citizen is one of the German people only. A German is a man of German blood, irrespective of his religious convictions. Therefore, no Jew can be one of the German people.

Art. 5: A non-citizen is allowed to live in Germany only as a guest, and must come under the jurisdiction of the Aliens Act.

Art. 8: Further immigration by non-Germans must be prohibited. All non-Germans who have entered the country since August 2, 1914 must be immediately expelled.

Art. 23b: Non-German newspapers may not publish without the explicit permission of the state. They may not be printed in the German language.

Art. 23c: Newspapers which do not act in the general interest will be forbidden. We demand a legal battle against any direction in the arts and literature which has a demoralizing influence on the life of our people, and the suppression of any gatherings which are contrary to the above requirements.

Art. 24: We demand freedom of religion for all religious creeds in the state, as long as their existence does not endanger the social and moral feelings of the German race. The party. . . fights against the materialistic Jewish spirit in and around us and is convinced that a lasting cure for our people can only come from the inside out according to the principle: general interest above private interest.

1921
Hitler becomes party leader of the NSDAP.

1923
Hitler tries to seize power in Germany, but his time has not yet come. His putsch is unsuccessful and he is thrown into prison, where he writes *Mein Kampf*.

1924-1932
Hitler is freed, in December, 1924. He meets with little political opposition in the next few years. The industrialists see in him a fighter against bolshevism and many support him; the Social Democrats are weak and divided among themselves. They believe that Hitler is better than he appears to be, although they see his political opponents swept ruthlessly out of the way by the Hitler Stormtroopers (SA). Terrorism begins. All demonstrations are used by the

Entry in Goebbels' Diary, October 26, 1925: "Saturday and Sunday were two days in which a lot happened. Went with the truck to Dortmund. A fight in the streets. With all that stirred up red rabble. We wounded forty-four. Crazy mess. Hitler isn't there. Had to arrest them. The room was jammed full. Streicher spoke like a pig. Blood flows. Doesn't matter."

An NSDAP functionary wrote: "The natural animosity of the farmer toward the Jew, his animosity toward the freemason as the servant of the Jew, must be worked up to a frenzy. These are the literal consequences of the lessons in 'Mein Kampf' in which Hitler himself gives his anti-Semitic feelings free rein."

Nazis to their own advantage. People point to the impotence in the government and the danger from the communists. Fear grips the population, pushed on and exploited by Goebbels, information director of the NSDAP.

In German universities in the '20s and '30s it was customary to beat up Jews and socialists. The police were not allowed to trespass on academic territory. They watched while Nazis mistreated, humiliated, spat upon, and even seriously wounded these students on the very steps of the university. When the Nazis abandoned their victims, they were pushed into waiting ambulances. A Catholic university teacher protested that these excesses were against academic dignity. After the roaring laughter had subsided, one of the Nazi ringleaders answered: "Why should we be ashamed? What happens here today will happen tomorrow everywhere in the country! Haven't you understood yet that we are the strongest, and that even you black robes will crawl to the cross — the hooked cross, the swastika!"

1933

Hindenburg makes Hitler Chancellor of State. No mention is made of the previously announced peace policy. The arms industry is set in motion. Pogroms begin.

Hitler used terror as a political weapon, first to gain power himself, then to eliminate his political opposition, and finally, to inspire fear in the German people.

Hitler: *Have you seen how a crowd assembles when two individuals are fighting in the street? Cruelty makes an impression. Cruelty, brute force, and ruthlessness impress! The women and children, too, for that matter. People need to have good healthy fear in them. They even want to be afraid of something. They want someone to make them afraid so that they can shudderingly submit themselves to a protector. Haven't you made the discovery everywhere that after disturbances at meetings, the ones who are first to give their names as new members of the Party are the very ones who have just been beaten up? Why do you chatter about cruelty and get excited about pain? That's what the masses want. They need something to shiver about.* (Conversation with Rauschnigg)

Berlin students hand out the following proclamation:

a) Language and literature are rooted in the people. . .

b) There is at present an antagonism between literature and the nature of the German people. This situation is defamatory.

c) Purity of language and literature lies in your hands.

d) Our most dangerous adversary is the Jew.

e) The Jew is only able to think like a Jew. When he writes German he is lying. The German who writes German but doesn't think German is a traitor. . .

f) We want to root out the lies; we want to brand the treason. . .

g) We consider the Jew a foreigner and take the character of our people seriously. Therefore, we demand censorship: Jewish works must appear in Hebrew. If they appear in German they must be indicated as translations. The German written language is only to be used by Germans. The non-German spirit must be removed from the public libraries.

The Nazis used every possible means to bring the German people to consider the Jew their great enemy. Latent anti-Semitism was formed into a powerful political weapon. Immediately after Hitler came to power, measures were taken to boycott the Jew and to ban him from public life. On May 21, 1933, thousands of books and magazines from homes, garages, cellars, and attics were confiscated and thrown into a bonfire to the cheers of crowds of Germans. The Horst-Wessel song, and "Deutschland, Deutschland über Alles," rang out again. The wave of destruction continued throughout the country. Goebbels called it a "powerful symbolic act."

During the Nazi regime countless synagogues went up in flames. Especially notorious is the "Kristallnacht" of 1938.

Otto Frank says:
"On January 30 we happened to be at the home of friends. We listened to the radio while we sat around the table. First we heard the shouting and cheering. Hindenburg stood at the window and waved, the announcer said. At the end Hitler said: 'Give me four years...' My host said in good spirits: 'Why don't we just see what the man can do? Give him a chance!'"

1935

March — General military conscription is reintroduced in Germany and open rearmament begins.

September — The anti-Jewish "Nuremberg Laws" are proclaimed.

1936

March — Hitler occupies the Rhineland.

1938

March 13 — Austria annexed.

October 1 — Occupation of the Sudetenland. England and France try to maintain peace in spite of the obvious injustice of these acts. Meanwhile, Hitler prepares for war.

1939

March 13 — Occupation of Czechoslovakia.

August 23 — Non-aggression pact between Germany and Russia.

September 1 — Invasion of Poland.

September 3 — France, England, and Canada declare war on Germany.

Public humiliation of the Jews in 1938.

Otto Frank was a banker when Hitler came to power in 1933 and the first anti-Jewish laws were published. Fortunes were confiscated, and the Jews were excluded from public life by a series of decrees. The population was asked to boycott Jewish business firms. The Stormtroopers began a wave of terrorism. On the 6th of March they swarmed through the streets, committed crimes of violence, and murdered hundreds of people. Concentration camps were constructed, and Jews came under the jurisdiction of the Gestapo. In addition, the Stormtroopers set up bunkers where communists were beaten. After several weeks, Goering abolished these free camps and put them under state supervision, explicitly under his command. Surrounding countries, no longer ignorant of the terrorism within Germany, protested. A retaliatory action directed at the Jews, of course, was prepared in answer to these protests.

About 80% of the Jewish population was living in Europe in 1900. From 1900 on, during the reawakening of anti-Semitism, many of them emigrated to America. In 1921 only 65% of the Jewish population was in Europe. In 1939 it was only 57%. After 1926, however, emigration to America decreased.

In 1933, after Jewish and non-Jewish children are forbidden to attend the same schools, Otto Frank flees to Holland.
Initially the Dutch borders are open for the Jews. About 6000 refugees are admitted by 1938, when the Dutch borders close.

On May 10, 1940, the Germans invade Holland. The country surrenders five days later.

Soon afterwards the first anti-Jewish measures are taken. In July all Dutch Jews are required to register, and in October Jewish businesses are required to register. Public officials have to sign the so-called "Arian statement."

In January, 1941, Jews are forbidden to attend the cinema, and a *numerus clausus* for Jewish students is introduced. Jewish professors are refused positions at universities. In February all Jewish professors are dismissed. After serious provocations by the NSB (Dutch Nazi Party), desperately resisted by Jewish and non-Jewish groups, the first raid on the Jews takes place on February 22. More than 400 young men are arrested and taken to a concentration camp.

Anti-Jewish regulations become more and more stringent. Jews are no longer allowed to visit parks or public swimming pools, and in October, 1941, the Jews are forbidden to practice a profession. No Jew is allowed to be director of a business. Consequently Mr. Frank transfers his to Mr. Koophuis. Jewish children are concentrated in Jewish schools. In April, 1942, the Jews are required to wear a "Jewish star" which must be easily recognizable on the outside of their clothing. This yellow star, which originated in medieval anti-Semitic proclamations, is purchased with "textile coupons." Food and clothing can be obtained only with these coupons, and the German distribution apparatus sends most of the supplies of food to Germany.

From February, 1942, many raids take place and, in July, the Frank family goes into hiding in the Annex.

Mr. Koophuis said about the raids:
...We tried to say nothing about what was happening outside. But it could not be concealed. The air was charged with it. It penetrated through the walls. Almost everything happened at night, you know, when we, too, were back at home. But we all heard the roar of the cars, the stopping, the pounding on the doors, heard it even in our beds. We could even hear the frightful ring of the bell, so exactly did we know what was happening. There were nights when you had the feeling that in all Amsterdam bells were ringing and fists pounding on doors.

Rauter to Himmler, September 24, 1952:
On the 15th of October Judaism was outlawed in Holland and anti-Semitic political action began. Not only the German and Dutch police organization took part, but also the members of the NSDAP, the NSB (the Dutch Nazi Party) the Wehrmacht, and other groups.
The storm which arose in the churches when the deportation began has abated. The Dutch police are newly united and do a good job. They arrest hundreds of Jews day and night. The only danger from them is that here and there a political official embezzles the goods of a Jew.

The artificially stimulated thirst for blood, this fighting spirit which called for "vengeance," was the basic German principle which Himmler, among others spoke about to his SS guards:
"I am now talking about the evacuation of the Jews, the extermination of the Jewish people... Most of you will know what it means when 100 corpses lie together, or 500 or 1000. To have endured this and — apart from human weaknesses — to have remained respectable, that has made us hard. That is a never written nor to be written page of triumph in our history.
"It is my concern to get rid of the Jews as soon as possible. That is not a great ideal but rather a great undertaking. The German SS will show no pity to the Jews as long as the German people stand behind them. He who doesn't understand this and talks about pity and humanism, cannot be a leader in this day and age."

Diary of Dr. Kremer — SS officer at Auschwitz 9-2-42 — For the first time I attended a special activity (a mass murder) at three o'clock in the morning. In comparison to this Dante's hell is a comedy.
9-5-42 — This afternoon I attended special activity at the women's camp. Army doctor Thilo was right when he told me today we were in the Anus Mundi. At eight o'clock this evening we were again at a special activity from Holland.
9-6-42 — Today we had an excellent lunch, tomato soup, half a chicken with potatoes and cabbage, some sweets and delicious ice cream. At 8 p.m. we attended a special activity.
9-9-42 — At night participated in a special activity (four times). How many people like me live in this world?

Number of victims of the main concentration camps.

Bergen-Belsen	50,000
Ravensbrück	92,000
Buchenwald	63,500
Dachau	70,000
Mauthausen	138,500
Flossenburg	74,000
Theresiënstadt	35,000
Sachsenhausen	100,000
Auschwitz	2,000,000
Maidenek	1,380,000
Belzec	600,000
Sobibor	280,000
Treblinka	731,800
Chelmno	600,000
Stuthof	67,500

The Origin of the Dairy

Professor L. De Jong
Executive Director of the Netherlands State Institute
for War Documentation in Amsterdam.

From *Reader's Digest*, October 1957.

"And how do you know that the human race is *worth* saving?" an argumentative youngster once asked Justice Felix Frankfurter. Said the Justice: "I have read Anne Frank's diary." How this diary of a teen-age girl came to be written and saved is a story as dramatic as the diary itself. No one foresaw the tremendous impact the small book would have — not even her father, who had it published after Anne's death in a Nazi concentration camp. *The Diary of Anne Frank* has now been published in 19 languages, including German, and has sold close to two million copies. Made into a play by Frances Goodrich and Albert Hackett, it won the Pulitzer Prize for Drama, and, in the 1956-1957 season alone, was shown in 20 different countries to two million people. Twentieth Century Fox is turning it into a film. To understand this amazing response it is necessary first to understand the girl who was Anne Frank.

When Hitler came to power, Otto Frank was a banker, living in Germany.[1] He had married in 1925.[2] In 1926 his first daughter, Margot, was born and three years later his second, Annelies Marie. She was usually called "Anne," sometimes "Tender one."

In the autumn of 1933, when Hitler was issuing one anti-Jewish decree after another, Otto Frank decided to emigrate to the hospitable Netherlands. He started a small firm in Amsterdam. Shortly before the outbreak of war he took in a partner, Mr. Van Daan, a fellow refugee. Mostly they traded in spices. Trade was often slow. Once Otto Frank was forced to ask his small staff to accept a temporary cut in their modest wages. No one left. They all liked his warm personality. They admired his courage and the evident care he took to give his two girls a good education.

As a pupil Anne was not particularly brilliant. Most people believed with her parents that Margot, her elder sister, was more promising. Anne was chiefly remarkable for the early interest she took in other people. She was emotional and strongwilled; "a real problem child," her father once told me, "a great talker and fond of nice clothes." Life in a town, where she was usually surrounded by a chattering crowd of girl friends, suited her exactly. This was a lucky fact because the Frank family could only rarely afford a holiday. Nor did they own a car.

When the Nazis invaded the Netherlands in May 1940, the Franks were trapped. Earlier than most Jews in Amsterdam, Otto Frank realized that the time might come when he and his family would have to go into hiding.

He decided to hide in his own business office, which faced one of Amsterdam's tree-lined canals. A few derelict rooms on the upper floors, called the "Annex," were secretly prepared to house both the Frank and the Van Daan families.

Early in July 1942, Margot Frank was called up for deportation, but she did not go. Straightway the Franks moved into their hiding place, and the Van Daans followed shortly afterward. Four months later they took into their cramped lodgings another Jew, a dentist.

They were eight hunted people. Any sound, any light might betray their presence. A tenuous link with the outside was provided by the radio and by four courageous members of Otto Frank's staff, two of them typists, who in secret brought food, magazines, books. The only other company they had was a cat.

While in hiding, Anne decided to continue a diary which her parents had given her on her thirteenth birthday. She described life in the "Annex" with all its inevitable tensions and quarrels. But she created first and foremost a wonderfully delicate record of adolescence, sketching with complete honesty a young girl's feelings, her longings and loneliness. *I feel like a songbird whose thoughts and wings have been brutally torn out and who is flying in utter darkness against the bars of its own cage*, she wrote when she had been isolated from the outside world for nearly 16 months. Two months later she had filled every page in the diary, a small book bound in a tartan cloth, and one of the typists, Miep, gave her an ordinary exercise book. Later she used Margot's chemistry exercise book. Her diary reveals the trust she put in her wise father; her grief because, as she feels it, her mother does not understand her; the ecstasy of a first, rapturous kiss, exchanged with the Van Daan's 17-year-old son; finally

the flowering of a charmingly feminine personality eager to face life with adult courage and mature self-insight.

On a slip of paper Anne wrote fake names which she intended to use in case of publication. For the time being the diary was her own secret which she wanted to keep from everyone, especially from the grumpy dentist with whom she had to share her tiny bedroom. Her father allowed her to put her diaries in his briefcase. He never read them until after her death.

On August 4, 1944, one German and four Dutch Nazi policemen suddenly stormed upstairs. (How the secret of the Annex had been revealed is not known.) "Where are your money and jewels?" they shouted. Mrs. Frank and Mrs. Van Daan had some gold and jewelry. It was quickly discovered. Looking around for something to carry it in, one of the policemen noticed Otto Frank's brief case. He emptied it on the floor, barely giving a glance to the notebooks. Then the people of the Annex were arrested.

In the beginning of September, while the Allied armies under Eisenhower were rapidly approaching the Netherlands, the Franks and the Van Daans and the dentist were carried in cattle-trucks to Auschwitz — the Nazi death camp in southern Poland. There the Nazis separated Otto Frank from his wife and daughters without giving them time to say farewell. Mrs. Frank, Anne, Margot were marched into the women's part of the camp, where Mrs. Frank later died from exhaustion. The Van Daans and the dentist also lost their lives.

Anne proved to be a courageous leader of her small Auschwitz group. When there was nothing to eat, she dared to go to the kitchen to ask for food. She constantly told Margot never to give in. Once she passed hundreds of Hungarian Gypsy children who were standing naked in freezing rain, waiting to be led to the gas chamber, unable to grasp the horrors inflicted upon them in the world of adults. "Oh look, their eyes," she whispered.

Later in the autumn she and her sister were transported to another camp, Bergen-Belsen, between Berlin and Hamburg. A close friend saw her there: "Cold and hungry, her head shaven and her skeleton-like form draped in the coarse, shapeless striped garb of the concentration camp." She was pitifully weak, her body racked by typhoid fever. She died in early March, 1945, a few days after Margot. Both were buried in a mass grave.

In Auschwitz Otto Frank had managed somehow to stay alive. He was freed early in 1945 by the Russians, and in the summer he returned to liberated Amsterdam. He knew that his wife had died, but he hoped that Anne and Margot would return. Six weeks later he met someone who told him that both had perished. It was then that Miep, his former typist, handed him Anne's diaries.

During the week after the Frank family had been arrested, Miep had boldly returned to the Annex. A pile of papers lay on the floor. Miep recognized Anne's handwriting and decided to keep the diary but not to read it. Had she read it, she would have found detailed information on the help she and other people had given the Frank family, and she might well have destroyed the diary for reasons of safety.

It took Otto Frank many weeks to finish reading the diary, so moved was he by what his dead child had written. He copied the manuscript for his mother, who had emigrated and was living in Switzerland with relatives. He left out some passages which he felt to be too intimate or which might hurt other people's feelings. The idea of publishing the diary did not enter his mind, but he wanted to show it to a few close friends. He gave one typed copy to a friend, who lent it to Jan Romein, a professor of modern history. Much to Otto Frank's surprise the professor devoted an article to it in a Dutch newspaper, *Het Parool*.

His friends now urged Otto Frank to have Anne's diary published as she herself had wished; in one passage she had written: *I want to publish a book entitled The Annex after the war. . .my diary can serve this purpose.*

Editor's Notes:
1 In Frankfurt-am-Main. His father came from an old German-Jewish family in the Rhineland and, on his mother's side, the family registers in Frankfurt go back to the 17th century.
2 To Edith Holländer from Aix-la-Chapelle.

Photos page 18: Mr. Otto Frank, Edith Frank, Margot Frank, Peter Van Daan, Mr. Dussel.
Photos page 19: Mrs. Van Daan, Mr. Van Daan, Mr. Kraler, Miep, Elli, Mr. Koophuis.

A Child's Voice

Jan Romein

Purely by chance a diary written during the war years has come into my hands. The Government Institute for War Documentation is in possession of about two hundred similar diaries, but it would amaze me if there was *one* among them as pure, as intelligent, and yet as human as this one. I read it from beginning to end without stopping, forgetting my many responsibilities for several hours. When I finished it was evening, and I was astonished that the light was burning, that there was still bread and tea, that I heard no airplanes droning above and no soldiers' boots shuffling on the streets, so thoroughly had this diary captured me and carried me back to the unreal world, behind us for almost a year now.

It was written by a Jewish girl, who was thirteen when she went into hiding with her parents and older sister and began this diary. It ended over two years later on the terrible day when the Gestapo discovered the family's hiding place. She died just before her sixteenth birthday in one of the worst German concentration camps, one month before the liberation.

I don't want to conjecture about how she died, but I am afraid her death was similar to those we read about in so many camp memoirs. Perhaps it was the same as that described in "Between Life and Death in Auschwitz," even though it happened in another camp.

The way she died is unimportant. More important is that this young life was willfully cut off by a system of irrational cruelty. We had sworn to each other never to forget or forgive this system as long as it was still raging, but now that it is gone, we too easily forgive, or at least forget, which ultimately means the same thing.

For me this apparently insignificant diary, this *de profundis* in the stammering voice of a child, embodies the real hideousness of fascism, more than all the trials of Nuremberg. For me the lot of this young girl sums up the worst crime of that abominable spirit. The worst crime is not the destruction of life and culture in itself; these things can also fall victim in a culture-creating revolution. The worst crime is the damming of the sources of culture, the destruction of life and talent only because of a senseless desire to destroy. If all signs do not deceive us, this girl, had she lived, would have become a talented writer. Coming to Holland at the age of four, she was able to write an enviably pure and sober Dutch ten years later, and she exhibited an insight into human nature — including her own — so faultless that it would be surprising in an adult, let alone a child. She also displayed, equally faultlessly, the limitless possibilities for humor, compassion, and love in human nature. These we should admire perhaps even more than her insight, and we might even shy away from them as we sometimes do from something very special, if her rejection and acceptance had not at the same time remained so profoundly childlike. That it was possible for this child to have been taken away and killed is proof for me that we have lost the battle against the beast in man.

We have lost because we have not been able to substitute something positive for it. And that is why we will lose again. No matter in what form inhumanity may lay traps for us, we will fall into them as long as we are unable to replace that inhumanity with a positive force.

The promise never to forget or forgive is not enough. It is not even enough to keep the promise. Passive and negative defense is almost the same as no defense.

Active, positive, total democracy — political, social, economic, and cultural democracy — is the only means by which we can build a society in which talent is no longer destroyed, oppressed, and driven out, but is discovered, cultivated, and encouraged wherever it may show itself.

And with all our good intentions, we are still as far away from this kind of democracy as we were before the war.

"A Child's Voice" was published in the Dutch newspaper "Het Parool," April 3, 1946. Written by the late Jan Romein, Professor of Dutch History at the University of Amsterdam, the article was the first serious attempt to evaluate Anne's diary as a historic document.

Anne received the first diary album for her thirteenth birthday. After the Frank family was deported, Miep and Elli found it, together with a family photograph album, two notebooks in which the diary was continued, 312 pages of notes from the diary, a notebook of stories written by Anne, and a book of quotations she had collected.

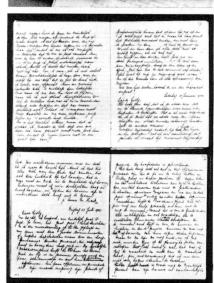

Anne Frank's Handwriting

Observations of the graphologist, Dr. Erhard W. Friess

From an article "Anne Frank's Selbstbeurteilung in graphologischer Sicht" in "Graphologisches Studienbuch," 1967.

General remarks

The very sensitive, impressionable author of this sample has a marked inclination toward an active life; the general appearance of the script in this regard bespeaks a quite special orientation that is intimately connected with the writer's overall character. External stimuli, positive and negative, easily disturb her equilibrium, but in the case of this highly kinetic character, that trait does not go so far as to produce chaos. Her excellent inner balance and notable control permit her to maintain strict discipline through the crises of life, and even in merely ticklish situations. Her great sensitivity and youthful temperament find conflict in many internal and external challenges; tension and mild overstrain arise, and, as it were, "spontaneous" friction with her surroundings (at least in part); out of all this a marked, and basically well-founded sense of superiority develops, and adds a slightly authoritarian note to the whole. Frequently, as a consequence of her highly intense nature, the boundaries set by circumstances or the claims of the ego itself are respected only up to a certain point. But thanks to her fundamentally healthy character and straightforward personality, most of her resolves and impulses are connected with ethical, sincere, honest, upright tendencies. There is often discernable in her character a pronounced instinct for giving definite shape and form to her imaginings. That instinct is spurred on by a very powerful desire for maturity, without sacrificing the best qualities of childhood — for Anne Frank as a child has a very genuine personality, one far removed from bluff or affectation. Whenever she reveals touches of willfulness, she is sure to counter them with self-criticism, keeping her strong impulses firmly within bounds without belying her powerful personality and charming character. The young writer is eager for education in the truest sense of the word. She is well aware herself that this strong tendency has no connection with submissiveness. It is rather a matter of her being so strict with herself that no strictness is required on the part of those who have the responsibility for her upbringing. Her ready cheerfulness is often at the service of her sense of discipline, reducing the pressures of circumstances so that there is room not merely for simple friendliness but for the most comradely feelings toward fellow beings in need of help. Indeed, from the very discipline she imposes on herself out of fidelity and faith, a compensating tendency arises that is directed to the social area — the more so because she is very much aware and has excellent powers of observation. And since these qualities are joined to a reflective disposition, naturalness, and a love of nature, the resulting highly developed sense of responsibility has a very special coloring of humanitarian concern.

Development and ripening of her character

Character development thus far has been natural, orderly, and normal. The possibilities for further development are very good, especially in the direction of the progressive enrichment of her personality. In part her stage of character maturation reflects the average for German girls of the same age; in part it far exceeds that average.

Intelligence, mental constitution

The gifted young author has at her disposition a mind that is above average, highly differentiated, lively, and empathetic. Much can be hoped for from her good habits of mental discipline. Her capacity for good judgment is apparent in her orderliness, clarity, accuracy, multiple relations, marked independence, thorough objectivity, and spiritedness; however, minor lapses of judgment are by no means excluded. It is quite unmistakable that her powers of imagination are far above average; these strike a good balance between a happy fantasy and compelling logic.

Photo taken in 1939, on Anne's 10th birthday, in front of the house on the Merwedeplein in Amsterdam. Anne is the second girl from the left, Sanne the third, and Lies the fourth (see *Diary* June 15, 1942). Kitty is the fourth girl from the right.

Zaterdag 12 Feb. 1944.

Lieve Kitty,

[handwritten diary entry in Dutch, signed] Je Anne.

The handwriting of Anne Frank

Dr. Mina Becker, a graphologist and psychologist from Hamburg, Germany, gave a lecture at the University of Amsterdam on March 8, 1962 for the Dutch Association for the Promotion of Scientific Graphology.

Dr. Becker was called in as an expert in 1960 in a legal case concerning the authenticity of the manuscript of "The Diary of Anne Frank." In Basel, in Otto Frank's home, she made a detailed analysis of Anne's handwriting.

Dr. Becker compared the handwriting in the diary itself with an abundance of material written by Anne during the same period of time. As a result she declared that the Diary was unquestionably an original manuscript, written by Anne Frank.

Her lecture was illustrated with slides of, among other things, a postcard from November 1940, when Anne was eleven years old, in a handwriting which seemed to be anything but that of a school girl, as well as the last postcard, from July, 1942, written just before the Frank family went into hiding.

According to Dr. Becker, Anne's personality had reached a maturity which one generally finds only in people of middle age. Of the many characteristics of Anne's handwriting, she stressed above all the loops which became increasingly more pointed. From the 60,000 children's letters she had analyzed after the war, she had deduced that this characteristic points specifically to a decline in physical health and a lack of physical activity and fresh air.

Ideas are Dynamite

The book that caused a chain reaction.

Henri van Praag

The sociologist Freyer has compared the physical concept of mass with the sociological concept of the mass. Both are sources of great energy, which can be used for constructive as well as for destructive purposes.

It is inaccurate to consider constructive as useful and destructive as detrimental. Some "constructive" activities are immoral and some destructive acts, such as the breakdown of prejudice, are of great value. One ought always to ask oneself what sort of goal one is pursuing when building up or tearing down.

It is also true that energy is used first for destructive purposes and only later for constructive projects. That applies to physical forces such as fire and atomic energy, but it also applies to spiritual fire, and the energy of the human personality.

Anne Frank's example has had a particularly volatile effect. It has kindled flames in the hearts of millions, and these flames have often exploded in deeds.

The Nazis burned innumerable Jewish books. But they overlooked one book written by a child. And now it is in bookstore windows throughout the world.

In Hebrew there is only one word for both spirit and wind: *ruach. The wind bloweth where it listeth,* says Jesus. It is this wind which has blown the diary of a school child over the whole world in order to extinguish the flames of tyranny.

How does it happen that a diary of a child has had such an extraordinary effect on mankind? The answer is, simply, that a child is the symbol of human perfection and purity. As Christ says in the gospel, *unless ye be as little children, ye shall not enter into the kingdom of heaven.* And the Chinese sage, Lao-tse also exhorts us to become like children again.

He who does not lose his child's heart can hope for a better world where peace and justice will prevail. But the modern world, with all its tensions and discord, puts terrible pressures on man. Even the child of today has difficulty remaining childlike, so bedeviled is he by news of chaos and violence, hate, hunger, and misery.

How surprising it is that a child, who herself had to suffer under the terror of Nazism and anti-Semitism, who lived in the shadow of death, could continue to believe in human goodness, in pure love, and in the victory of right over wrong and willful, senseless destruction, that this young Jewish girl was convinced that the suffering of the Jews had a deeper meaning and would contribute to the realization of a world without discrimination.

Anne Frank inspires us to keep our child's heart. Even in the concentration camp she helped other children who were to die. Her sense of solidarity with mankind is stronger than all the powers of brute violence. For real humanity is a charge of dynamite, by which the bulwarks of hate and intolerance will be demolished in the end.

And so it appears again as it has so many times in history that ideas are dynamite. One can imagine them to be safely locked away, but it only takes a spark to ignite them.

The Legend and Art of Anne Frank

Henry F. Pommer

Few, if any personal documents emerging out of the Hitler years have had a wider appeal or more profound impact than the diary written in an Amsterdam garret by a girl in her early teens. It is reported that German audiences viewed the film version in stunned silence and left the theaters, after the showing, confused, ashamed, and humbled.

The elements of the book's appeal, as well as the figure of its young author, concern the writer of this essay. Dr. Henry F. Pommer is Associate Professor of English at Allegheny College (Meadville, Pa.) and is the author of *Milton* and *Melville* and a frequent contributor to such journals as *The Modern Churchman*, *Friends Journal*, and *The Crane Review*.

This article was originally published in *Judaism, a Quarterly Journal of Jewish Life and Thought* in the winter of 1960.

May 1935
December 1935

On an unrecorded date in March, 1945, Anne Frank succumbed to the malnutrition, exposure, typhus, and despair of the Bergen-Belsen concentration camp. She was back in her native Germany because her family had not fled far enough in 1933, going only to Amsterdam. And she was back because the Allies had not advanced fast enough in the summer of '44; the long train of freight cars which on September 3 took Anne to Germany was the last shipment of Jews to leave Holland. It moved on the day that Brussels was freed by the Allies.

The quality of both her death and her life have given Anne Frank an extraordinary status in our culture. Antigone represents a willingness to die for principles; Juliet's is the tragedy of ironic confusion; Marguerite was the victim of her own and Faust's sensuality; St. Joan was martyred by jealous institutions. Anne was destroyed by a pattern of evil perhaps not unique to our century, but at least unique within Western culture of the past two thousand years.

But her fame rests on knowledge of her life as much as of her death. She is not a fictional character like Juliet or Tolstoy's Natasha, nor a girl with widespread and immediate influence like St. Joan or the young Cleopatra. Yet she shares with Cleopatra and St. Joan the fact of being historical; and her life is already, like theirs, the source of a legend. As an historical figure relatively unimportant to her immediate contemporaries but affecting a larger and larger circle after her death, she is most like St. Thérèse of Lisieux. But over all these girls from Antigone to St. Thérèse, Anne has the great advantage that she left a diary. Therefore, we need not know her through the documents of her contemporaries or the professional imagination of middle-aged authors. Her legend lacks the support of patriotic and ecclesiastical power, but it has the strength of her authentic, self-drawn portrait.

The legend she founded is the kind her destroyers had tried to wipe out. She is a Jewess spoken of by Germans as a saint; she was an object of hatred, and has become a vehicle of love.

Anne has been the object of research leading to a careful biography which suggests that "had she any premonition of the legend, had she been able to foresee that she would really live, would be far more real than ever the Anne Frank of life had been, she would have been alarmed to the very depths of her heart."

The legend had its start when the Nazi sergeant who arrested the Franks needed something in which to carry the money and valuables he was confiscating. He chose Anne's briefcase, and emptied her papers and notebooks on the floor. It was a fortunate event, for Anne was then less likely to take the papers with her, and they could lie unmolested a few days until Miep and Elli, loyal Dutch friends, found them and locked them up in Mr. Frank's former office. There the papers stayed until the return of Otto Frank, the only one of Anne's fellow fugitives to survive the concentration camps.

It took him many weeks to finish reading the diary; the emotional strain of even a few pages would overcome him. Eventually he copied out almost the entire work, omitting only "some passages which he felt to be too intimate or which might hurt other people's feelings." He had no thought of publishing it. But friends urged him to make it public; a Dutch professor published an article, based on one of the copies circulating privately; and finally the first edition appeared, in Holland.

Some writers have considered the diary as primarily "one of the most moving stories that anyone, anywhere, has managed to tell about World War II." At Oradoursur-Glane, where Nazis wantonly destroyed the entire population, is printed "Remember," and in the ruins of bomb-destroyed Coventry has been carved "Father Forgive." Anne's diary helps us remember what there is to forgive.

She reminds us that Amsterdam has not always been the peaceful and comfortable city we visit as summer tourists. On Sunday, July 5, 1942, the S.S. sent a notice that Margot Frank must report for forced labor. Early the next day, the entire family went into hiding, and in October Anne wrote that:

. . .our many Jewish friends are being taken away by the dozen. These people are treated by the Gestapo without a shred of decency, being loaded into cattle trucks and sent to Westerbork, the big Jewish camp in Drente. . .

It is impossible to escape; most of the people in the camp are branded as inmates by their shaven heads and many also by their Jewish appearance.

If it is as bad as this in Holland, whatever will it be like in the distant and barbarous regions they are sent to? We assume that most of them are murdered. The English radio speaks of their being gassed.

Perhaps that is the quickest way to die. I feel terribly upset. I couldn't tear myself away while Miep told these dreadful stories; and she herself was equally wound up for that matter. Just recently, for instance, a poor old crippled Jewess was sitting on her doorstep; she had been told to wait there by the Gestapo, who had gone to fetch a car to take her away. The poor old thing was terrified by the guns that were shooting at English planes overhead, and by the glaring beams of the searchlights. But Miep did not dare take her in; no one would undergo such a risk.

Yet Miep and her fellow Dutch conspirators did undergo such a risk for the Franks and the Van Daans and for Mr. Dussel, who joined Anne's group in November, bringing *. . .very sad news. Countless friends and acquaintances have gone to a terrible fate. Evening after evening the green and gray army lorries trundle past. The Germans ring at every front door to inquire if there are any Jews living in the house. If there are, then the whole family has to go at once. . .*

Often they go around with lists, and only ring when they know they can get a good haul. Sometimes they let them off for cash, so much per head. It seems like the slave hunts of olden times. . . In the evenings when it's dark, I often see rows of good, innocent people accompanied by crying children, walking on and on, in charge of a couple of these chaps, bullied and knocked about, until they almost drop. No one is spared: old people, babies, expectant mothers, the sick, each and all join in the march of death.

These were not, of course, the deeds of all Germans, but of the Nazis. Many Nazis were German, some were Dutch. The police sergeant who arrested the Franks, the Gestapo chief in the Netherlands, the Reich commissioner in the Hague, Hitler himself — all these were native Austrians; but so, too, were Miep and the equally loyal Mr. Kraler. As Anne's biographer says, "The dark line is not a line around nations. It runs right through nations."

If the Nazis' deeds are to be remembered as well as forgiven, the deeds of many non-Jewish Dutch are to be remembered as well as admired. During the seventeenth century René Descartes had lived in a house which Anne could see from her Secret Annex; there he had written about Holland, "Is there any other country in which one can enjoy freedom as one does here?" And Anne told her diary, *It is not the Dutch people's fault that we are having such a miserable time.* Some Dutch did, of course, cooperate with the Nazis; the hiders recognized two alternatives if they were discovered by Dutch police: "They would either be good Dutch people, then we'd be saved," or members of the Dutch National Socialist Movement, and then the fugitives would have to try bribery. And probably it was a Dutch citizen who finally betrayed the Franks. Yet against the small number of these collaborators stand the loyal friends and strangers who helped them at the cost of money, time, and comfort, and at the risk of death. For example, in the play Anne very briefly mentions a vegetable man. He lives in the diary as an unnamed grocer who came to suspect the presence of fugitives the warehouse, delivered potatoes to the Dutch staff at the least conspicuous times, and was alert enough once to scare burglars from the warehouse without calling the police. He was later arrested for harboring two Jews in his own house. His tact and his willingness to expose himself are symptomatic of a great many Dutchmen's deeds — deeds which were some of the most heroic of the war.

All these deeds deserve to be remembered because the truths of Anne's history,

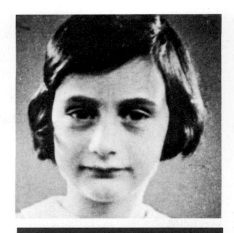

May 1936

May 1937
May 1938
May 1939

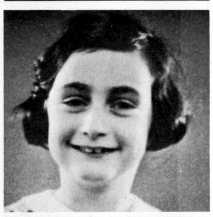

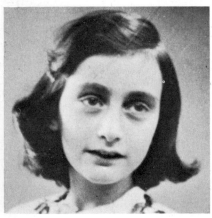

the bitter as well as the sweet, are not about Germans alone, or Dutchmen or Jews, but humanity. And these truths must be recalled whenever we try to measure human nature, to estimate its heights and depths, its capacities for good and evil. The extremes of cruelty temper all our hopes. On the other hand, a young person is supposed to have once asked Justice Felix Frankfurter, "And how do you know that the human race is *worth* saving?" The Justice replied, "I have read Anne Frank's diary."

A second group of critics has praised the diary as primarily an intimate account of adolescence. For these it is of only secondary importance that Anne hid with her family in an attic of old Amsterdam; of primary importance is her frankness in telling what it is like to grow up. Thus, an American teacher writes that "Anne's diary has given me a deeper understanding of the heart of adolescence than all my college education courses and all my years teaching young people." One reviewer of the first American edition called Anne's romance with Peter "the very type and model of early love;" another wrote that Anne had "succeeded in communicating in virtually perfect, or classic, form the drama of puberty." Norbert Muhlen has reported that Anne conquered "many young people, particularly in Germany. . . because they could identify themselves with her and her problems, different though they may seem. They discovered the image of their own suffering and their own search for the good life in Anne's extreme situation, as she lived and described it." Anne was thirteen when she started her diary. Six months later she regretted not having had her first menstruation. *I'm so longing to have it too,* she wrote, *it seems so important.* She tried to bleach her black moustache hairs with hydrogen peroxide; she collected pictures of film stars and hung them around her room. She betrayed further immaturity by remarking about Margot, *She lacks the nonchalance for conducting deep discussions.*

Often she was difficult to live with. Tensions were almost inevitable for eight people living with so many restrictions in such cramped quarters, but Anne seems to have done more than her share to stir up ill will. She had a temper, and was not always either anxious or able to control it. At times she must have been obnoxiously precocious in telling the other fugitives what they were like; she may have appeared very patronizing at times, particularly in dealing with Margot about Peter. She was very critical of her mother, very fond of her father, and from time to time hurt both of them deeply. Her sense of justice, her loathing of whatever was pompous or artificial, and her desire to be treated as an adult led to frequent quarrels with Mr. and Mrs. Van Daan, and with Mr. Dussel.

Bit by bit, however, these evidences of immaturity and of being difficult decreased. Mixed with them, yet gradually replacing them, came the actions and reactions of a more mature young woman. Probably the most striking measure of these changes is her love affair with Peter Van Daan. Before she went into hiding she had delighted in the company of many boys and had developed considerable self-conscious skill in handling them. As she settled down in the Secret Annex, she decided that Peter was completely uninteresting — *a rather soft, shy, gawky youth; can't expect much from his company.* But during the next eighteen months Anne's need for a confidant of her own age greatly increased, and she had her first period. Finally, on January 6, 1944, *my longing to talk to someone became so intense that somehow or other I took it into my head to choose Peter. . .*

Peter has a mania for crossword puzzles at the moment and hardly does anything else. I helped him with them and we soon sat opposite each other at his little table, he on the chair and me on the divan.

It gave me a queer feeling each time I looked into his deep blue eyes, and he sat there with that mysterious laugh playing around his lips. I was able to read his inward thoughts. I could see on his face that look of helplessness and uncertainty as to how to behave, and, at the same time, a trace of his sense of manhood. I noticed his shy manner and it made me feel very gentle; I couldn't refrain from meeting those dark eyes again and again, and with my whole heart I almost beseeched him: Oh, tell me, what is going on inside you, oh, can't you look beyond this ridiculous chatter?

But the evening passed and nothing happened. . .

When I lay in bed and thought over the whole situation, I found it far from encouraging, and the idea that I should beg for Peter's patronage was simply repellent. One can do a lot to satisfy one's longings, which certainly sticks out in my case, for I have made up my mind to go and sit with Peter more often and to get him talking somehow or other.

May 1940
May 1941

The first half of the diary records the nineteen months preceding this passage; the second half records with much greater detail the seven months that followed. They were for Anne far happier months than the earlier ones; parts of them were rapturous, even though visiting Peter's room as often as she wanted brought opposition and ridicule from the adults, even though being in love intensified her desire to be free, and even though she finally found Peter somewhat disappointing. He returned her love; he never stopped treating her affectionately; but as even Anne came to realize, he was not, in spite of his two and a half extra years, sufficiently mature to satisfy her emotional and intellectual needs. Anne had fallen in love with an ideal created by her needs; after a while it was disappointing to hold hands and talk with a mere Peter Van Daan.

Whatever their relationship was for Peter, for Anne it was a flood of new feelings, new problems, new insights concerning herself and other people; it helped her on the road to maturity. But other traits and experiences also helped — particularly her intellectualism and humor, her religious sense and courage, her capacity for self-analysis.

Shortly before she went into hiding, and while the teachers of her school were deciding whom to promote, Anne recorded her opinion that *a quarter of the class should stay where they are; there are some absolute cuckoos, but teachers are the greatest freaks on earth.* This may be evidence of her maturity or immaturity, her humor or her love of learning. In any event, it is clear from the rest of her diary that her cultured father reared her in the best European and Jewish traditions of education, so that Anne acquired not only a considerable amount of learning, but also a considerable love of it. Lessons continued regularly during the underground period, and everybody read. Anne studied French, Latin, and English; mathematics and algebra; geography, shorthand, history, and ballet. Books were important presents on each birthday, and through friends the fugitives used the public library. Anne justifiably described herself as having "a real appetite for learning."

She also had an appetite for humor. Hers was no doubt often immature, for example, when she wrote that *Mrs. Van Daan nags us the whole day long about the bad weather. It really would be nice to dump her in a bucket of cold water and put her up in the loft.* At times humor failed her completely. More frequently a mask of it protected her sensitive self from supercilious probing by adults; and she recorded *one golden rule to keep before you: laugh about everything and don't bother yourself about the others! It sounds selfish, but it's honestly the only cure for anyone who has to seek consolation in himself.*

Her humor, like her love for Peter, helped make her situation much better than merely bearable. So did her religious sentiment, which appears to have deepened during the months of hiding. The Franks were not Orthodox Jews. In their home they had not observed the ritual of the Sabbath; Anne and her father had attended synagogue only on high holidays, although Mrs. Frank and Margot attended regularly. During the period of hiding, Anne prayed each night. She prayed for miracles to save at least some of the Jews not fortunate enough to be in hiding; after scares which caused the fugitives to think they had been discovered, she thanked God for having protected them. At times her religious sentiment contained clear marks of the Old Testament, as when she asked:

Who has inflicted this upon us? Who has made us Jews different from all other people? Who has allowed us to suffer so terribly up till now? It is God that has made us as we are, but it will be God, too, who will raise us up again. If we bear all this suffering and if there are still Jews left, when it is over, then Jews, instead of being doomed, will be held up as an example. Who knows, it might even be our religion from which the world and all peoples learn good, and for that reason, and that reason only, do we have to suffer now.

Other expressions of religion suggest a Wordsworthian reliance on nature:

The best remedy for those who are afraid, lonely, or unhappy is to go outside, somewhere where they can be quite alone with the heavens, nature, and God. Because only then does one feel that all is as it should be and that God wishes to see people happy, amidst the simple beauty of nature. As long as this exists, and it certainly always will, I know that there will always be comfort for every sorrow, whatever the circumstances may be. And I firmly believe that nature brings solace in all troubles.

It is hardly surprising that Anne, together with her sense of humor and religious sentiment, had an abundance of courage. She wrote that *he who has courage and faith will never perish in misery,* and we can only hope that the statement was true of her to the end. She also wrote, *I have often been downcast, but never in despair; I regard our hiding as a dangerous adventure, romantic and interesting at the same time.* She made plans for her career after liberation, thought about the children she might bear, hoped for visits to Paris and London. Sometimes, to be sure, she found it difficult to imagine that liberation might occur, but most of the time optimism prevailed. And her expressions of courage and hopefulness must have been to the other fugitives a generous compensation for the stings her tongue inflicted at other times.

Any diary of a young girl who hid in Amsterdam during the Nazi occupation, who described her first protracted love affair, and who was a person of breeding, humor, religious sensitivity, and courage might well interest us. But Anne had one further trait of the utmost importance for her own maturity and for what she wrote: an unusual ability for self-analysis. She knew she had moods, and she could write eloquently about them — about loneliness, for example. But she could also step outside her moods in order to evaluate them and herself in them. Miep, having read the diary after the war, said that Anne described Mr. Dussel *with extreme severity;* Anne herself wrote, *Now the trying part about me is that I criticize and scold myself far more than anyone else does.* In an early entry she wrote, *I must become good through my own efforts;* a little later, *I must tell you that I am trying to be helpful, friendly, and good, and to do everything I can so that the rain of rebukes dies down to a light summer drizzle. It is mighty difficult to be on one's best behavior with people you can't bear, especially when you don't mean a word of it. But I do really see that I get on better by shamming a bit, instead of my old habit of telling everyone exactly what I think (although no one ever asked my opinion or attached the slightest importance to it).*

One of the clearest evidences of objectivity was her ability to see a moral ambiguity in her enjoying relative security while other Jews suffered worse fates.

I saw two Jews through the curtain yesterday. I could hardly believe my eyes; it was a horrible feeling, just as if I'd betrayed them and was now watching them in their misery.

This is the honesty concerning oneself out of which are born humor, maturity, and one kind of ability to write well.

Anne could write well. Her self-consciousness and skill as an author receive only implicit acknowledgment if we regard her diary as no more than an educative historical document or an intimate disclosure of adolescence. W. A. Darlington is probably correct in predicting that "in time to come, when the horrors of Nazi occupation in Europe are no longer quite so fresh in quite so many minds and "The Diary of Anne Frank" comes to be judged on its merits as a play, the piece will. . . lose its place on the stage."

But Anne's diary may have a longer life. It is, to be sure, a mixture of good and bad writing, but so, too, are the diaries of Pepys, Samuel Sewall, and William Byrd.

Some people have combed the external record of Anne's life for evidence of her ability as a writer. They have found very little. One of her early teachers remembers that she wanted to be a writer. "It started early with her, very early. . . She was able to *experience* more than other children, if you know what I mean. I might almost put it that she heard more, the soundless things too, and sometimes she heard things whose very existence we have almost forgotten." Mrs. Kuperus, who taught Anne a few years later, recalls that Anne "was full of ideas for the scripts" of plays which pupils wrote and produced during class. But she also recalls that "the compositions Anne wrote in school were just ordinary, no better than average. Many pupils wrote with more imagination and feeling than Anne. I've re-read the diary many times looking for clues to the amazing transformation in her, but I still don't know what caused it." Anne's friend, Lies Goossens, is surely correct in saying that the transformation was caused by "a combination of things in long hours of enforced reflection, the tragic intensity of the situation in which she and her family were living, and the flowering of her own physical maturity and her first love."

It was to be expected that little external evidence of Anne's talent would be found. When she went into hiding, she was not a diarist worthy of much attention. During the twenty-five months in the Secret Annex, the world of her thought was a secret within a secret, a secret so well kept that even her father confessed, when the diary was first published, "I never realized my little Anna was so deep."

After she had left the Annex, the brutality of guards, shortages of food, epidemics of disease, separation from loved ones, and the prospect of gas chambers must have left Anne little time to think about writing, and certainly gave her companions little interest in what her literary talents might be. Ever so much more important was whether she could beg a piece of bread.

When we turn to the diary itself, we find that if her affair with Peter is the most striking measure of her change towards maturity, the second most striking is the clarification of her desire to be a writer. The third entry begins the development.

I haven't written for a few days, because I wanted first of all to think about my diary. It's an odd idea for someone like me to keep a diary; not only because I have never done so before, but because it seems to me that neither I — nor for that matter anyone else — will be interested in the unbosomings of a thirteen-year-old schoolgirl. Still, what does that matter? I want to write, but more than that, I want to bring out all kinds of things that lie buried deep in my heart. . .

There is no doubt that paper is patient and as I don't intend to show this. . . "diary" to anyone unless I find a real friend, boy or girl, probably nobody cares. And now I come to the root of the matter, the reason for my starting a diary: it is that I have no such real friend. . .

It's the same with all my friends, just fun and joking, nothing more. I can never bring myself to talk of anything outside the common round. . .

Hence, this diary. In order to enhance in my mind's eye the picture of the friend for whom I have waited so long, I don't want to set down a series of bald facts in

May 1942

a diary as most people do, but I want this diary itself to be my friend, and I shall call my friend Kitty.

After this early entry, the diary shows a progressively self-conscious artistry reflected in the beginnings of certain letters to Kitty, such as:

Now that we have been in the "Secret Annex" for over a year, you know something of our lives, but some of it is quite indescribable. . . . To give you a closer look. . . , now and again I intend to give you a description of an ordinary day. Today I'm beginning with the evening and the night. . . . (August 4, 1943).

I asked myself this morning whether you don't sometimes feel rather like a cow who has had to chew over all the old pieces of news again and again, and who finally yawns loudly and silently wishes that Anne would occasionally find something new. . . . (January 28, 1944).

Perhaps it would be entertaining for you, though not in the least for me, to hear what we are going to eat today. . . (March 14, 1944).

That her diary might itself be the basis of a published work may not have occurred to Anne before March 29, 1944, when Bolkestein, an M. P., was speaking on the Dutch News from London, and said that they ought to make a collection of diaries and letters after the war. Of course, they all made a rush at my diary immediately. Just imagine how interesting it would be if I were to publish a novel about the "Secret Annex." The title alone would be enough to make people think it was a detective story.

But seriously, it would seem quite funny ten years after the war if we Jews were to tell how we lived and what we ate and talked about here.

It cannot have been long after this that Anne wrote out a list of fictitious names to be substituted for real ones if her diary were ever published — a list which Otto Frank used, changing, for example, the real name Van Pelz to Van Daan.

After the entry of March 29, Anne's expressed desire to be a journalist, and then a famous writer, grew more numerous. Writing would, she hoped, enable her to live after her death; she wrote short stories, even wanting to submit them for publication. Do You Remember?, a collection of fables and little personal experiences, was published in Holland after the diary and has become "something of a minor children's classic." In 1959 its contents become available in English in The Works of Anne Frank. But certainly the diary will live the longest: immature touches which are signs of authenticity are blemishes in the tales.

The chief literary merit of the diary is that it permits us to know intimately Anne's young, eager, difficult, lovable self. We follow the quick alternations of her great depression, and we benefit from the introspection generated by her sharply contrasting moods. Some pages read as though they had been written in the security of a Long Island suburb; on the next page we are plunged into Nazi terror; and both passages use vivid details. Sometimes our delight is simply in her charm, as in Daddy always says I'm prudish and vain but that's not true. I'm just simply vain. At other times her wisdom surprises us, as in her distinction that laziness may appear attractive, but work gives satisfaction. She sensed the need for variety in reporting, and used effective techniques for achieving it. Life in the Secret Annex was terribly repetitious, but there is little repetition in the diary itself.

Even if the last entry told of Jews liberated by the arrival of Allied armies in Amsterdam, the book would still have real interest and value. And it would still have its chief moral significance. Both diary and play illustrate D. H. Lawrence's contention that: ". . .the essential function of art is moral. Not aesthetic, nor decorative, not pastime and recreation. But moral. . . A passionate, implicit morality, not didactic. A morality which changes the blood, rather than the mind. Changes the blood first. The mind follows later in the wake."

Because of Anne Frank's art, this change in blood and then in mind sometimes takes the direction of brotherhood. At those moments her legend receives fresh life, and her adolescent record of history helps to make history less adolescent.

Prefaces to the Diary

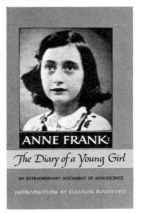

Under the exceptional circumstances of life in the Annex, the growth of the lively, intelligent and impressionable child Anne Frank, from girl to woman, from child to adult, occurred in a remarkably brief time. The relationship of the growing young individual to the outside world, which in normal life is recorded in a great number of more or less fluctuating and varying lines, was here reduced to an extremely simple pattern, forcing her perceptive spirit to expand in depth rather than in width. In a continual process of rapprochement, collision, and wrestling with the seven people around her, in a constant state of inquisitive examination of these seven eternal close-ups, the child's knowledge of human character grew perceptibly. Through introspection forced upon her by circumstances, through a struggle with herself and her limited possibilities, the self-knowledge of the child playing at keeping a diary, evolved with unbelievable speed to sharp analysis, even of her own dreams and illusions, of her reactions to her surroundings, of her fate, and of her abandonment of all the beautiful little girl's dreams which were no longer a part of her life in hiding.

Is it the isolation of the Annex, is it the dark uncertainty of the future, which makes this diary so pure in its conversation with itself, without one disturbing or unspontaneous thought of later readers? It lacks even a faraway echo of the remaining undertones of the diary by Marie Bashkirtsev: the desire to please. It is only necessary to study a bit of modern psychology to know that the years of our youth have enormous influence on our later attitudes toward life. One only has to look at the number of the very greatest writers who continually strive to disentangle their childhood from their mellowed or embittered memories. There is much more to say about this diary. It is a war document, a document of the cruelty and heartbreaking misery of the persecution of the Jews, of human helpfulness and treason, of human adjustment and non-adjustment, of the small joys and the great and small miseries of life in hiding, written in a direct, non-literary, and therefore often excellent style, by this child who in any case possessed the one important characteristic of a great writer: an open mind, untouched by complacency and prejudice.

But for me the most important thing about this diary is not the documentation, which so often is and will be recorded elsewhere. When people in the tropics take a young plant from the temperate mountain zone and plant it in a very hot area, it will bloom once, richly and superabundantly, only to die soon after. That feeling is what touches me the most in this diary.

In the same way, this small, plucky geranium stood and bloomed, and bloomed, behind the shuttered windows of the Annex.

Annie Romein-Verschoor, from the preface to the Dutch edition, "Het Achterhuis."

This is a remarkable book. Written by a young girl — and the young are not afraid of telling the truth — it is one of the wisest and most moving commentaries on war and its impact on human beings that I ever read. Anne Frank's account of the changes wrought upon eight people hiding out from the Nazis for two years during the occupation of Holland, living in constant fear and isolation, imprisoned not only by the terrible outward circumstances of war but inwardly by themselves, made me intimately and shockingly aware of war's greatest evil — the degradation of the human spirit.

At the same time, Anne's diary makes poignantly clear the ultimate shining nobility of that spirit. Despite the horror and the humiliation of their daily lives, these people never gave up. Anne herself — and, most of all, it is her portrait which emerges so vividly and so appealingly from this book — matured very rapidly in these two years, the crucial years from thirteen to fifteen in which change is so swift and so difficult for every young girl. Sustained by her warmth and her wit, her intelligence and the rich resources of her inner life, Anne wrote and thought much of the time about things which very sensitive and talented adolescents without the threat of death will write — her relations with her parents, her developing self-awareness, the problems of growing up.

These are the thoughts and expressions of a young girl living under extraordinary conditions, and for this reason her diary tells us much about ourselves and about our own children. And for this reason, too, I felt how close we all are to Anne's experience, how very much involved we are in her short life and in the entire world.

Anne's diary is an appropriate monument to her fine spirit and to the spirits of those who have worked and are working still for peace. Reading it is a rich and rewarding experience.

Eleanor Roosevelt, Introduction to the American edition "Anne Frank: The Diary of a Young Girl."

Now and then in the course of our life we meet a girl like Anne Frank — not too often, for the level of intelligence, reflectiveness, depth of feeling, and precocity that are revealed in the jottings of this thirteen- or fourteen-year-old are certainly extraordinary. But her cool, keen observation of human beings, and her resolve to be alert to the comic element in even the worst situations, these are familiar to us: they belong to the armor worn by our generation.

We have her diary still, and in that journal a most remarkable document of awakening humanity written down quite without premeditation, and for that very reason absolutely sincere.

It is a dialogue between one "I" and another, between a highly sensitive, thinskinned being and another that seems to be armed with thorns. And it is a dialogue between the one "I" and the surrounding world, a discussion carried on with painstaking exactitude. No one could possibly miss the aggressive note that dominates the dialogue, and no one could miss the second tone that is not dominant and yet is the true keynote of the whole: the note of a genuine ability to love. If the reader is inclined to wonder that we dare to speak of the ability to love in this context, when we are dealing with observations written down by a child — well, there is ample ground for wonder in this book. But at least we must testify that the dialogue between the "I" and the world, set down in these pages, is carried on with a most uncommon instinct for reaching its appointed goal. This young person who loves and hates and struggles and suffers, knows what objectives she must strive towards, what answer is demanded of her by the claims of the hour and those of the nation, which for Anne Frank is Holland — and Israel.

More than a decade has passed now, and life in Amsterdam's Prinsengracht runs its course, as it does everywhere, runs its lively and forgetful course. It is necessary that this voice be heard in the world of 1955, which has not ceased to be a world of concentration camps and persecutions. And one must be ever grateful to the two Hollanders who, in that room ransacked by the Secret Police, hid and kept secure under magazines and newspapers this child's journal — this book that tells the truth without a trace of false ornament, tells the whole truth and nothing but the truth.

Albrecht Goes, from the preface to the German edition of the diary, Das Tagebuch der Anne Frank.

... This book is a diary, and I can well understand, that the very word is enough to arouse suspicion. A child of thirteen writing her diary. Childishness? Dreadful precocity? Neither one nor the other... Anne Frank's daily notations are so modest in tone, so true, that it never occurs to a reader that she might have written them with any "literary" motive — still less that a "grown-up" might have revised them. From beginning to end one is convinced of their unquestionable authenticity. If the word did not connote something dusty and discolored, one would be tempted to call the book a document.

Daniel Rops, from the preface to the French edition of the diary, Journal de Anne Frank.

The Diary as Drama

Henri van Praag

The historical origin of theater and film is religious drama. In this drama the myth of a religious society was told and retold on the stage.

In biblical religion basic spiritual truths were not just repeated, but had to be fulfilled in history. When they are acted out, as in the Jewish Passover and Purim celebrations, the mass, and passions plays, it is to keep their memory alive from generation to generation. If the myth should ever become lost in the dramatization, the historical task would remain uncompleted. That is why synagogues and churches in our time emphasize the church's mission in the world, and secularization as a religious task. Abraham Joshua Heschel's *The Earth is the Lord's* and Harvey Cox's *The Secular City* are striking examples of this.

Looking at the play based on Anne Frank's diary in this light, one notices that many people today experience these dramatizations as modern cult plays. Others see them as historical drama and still others think of them as symbolic. The play, which is performed still regularly in many countries, fulfills the role of social drama, in which the young actors strongly identify themselves with the characters in the diary.

How should a sociologist describe the diary as a scenario? This can, of course, be done in more than one way. One should, however, ask oneself in which way the spirit of the diary is best served; as a cult play or as a social drama, as a reminder of the past or as a morality play, as realistic or symbolic. To answer these questions a number of things must first be clarified.

A visit to Amsterdam by the authors of the theatrical script of The Diary of Anne Frank. In front of the Anne Frank House, from left to right: Mr. Koophuis, Mrs. Elfriede Frank-Markovits, Mrs. Frances Goodrich Hackett, Mr. Albert Hackett, Mr. Otto Frank, and Mr. Garson Kanin (director of the play in New York).

Susan Strasberg and Joseph Schildkraut in the first theatrical performance, New York City, October 5, 1955.

The myth of the diary

The objection has often been raised that propaganda and publicity for the diary create a new myth which helps people to sublimate their guilt feelings under cheap sentimentality. This makes both the escape from reality and the evasion of historical responsibility easier to achieve.

Since this complaint is often made by people of unquestionable good faith, who have themselves worked to make the diary known to the world, we must examine this criticism carefully. This is even more true because we have, in our times, been witness to the disastrous effects of the exploitation of a myth which attracted the imagination of millions, the myth of Nazism.

It will be clear to the reader that we do not mean here by "myth" a primitive or antique story of the gods, but a fundamental religious concept, underlying a culture or movement. And no culture can exist without myths. Educators and statesmen stimulate the development of beneficial myths. As Churchill said: "A politican thinks about the next election, a statesman thinks about the next generation."

The history of National Socialism, of which Anne Frank was one of the millions of victims, has proved that demoniacal myths take hold where humane myths are lacking.

According to the views of the leading sociologists and religious historians (Van der Leeuw, Werblowsky, Kerenyi and the like) a myth only becomes suspect if it distorts authentic history (as did Fascism) or if it is based on a negative choice as is racism). When moral achievement is the basis of the myth — as is the case with the diary — that moral achievement can be amplified through the myth, to the salvation of all those who see it as a shining example. The death of Socrates still represents a powerful testimony that it is better to suffer injustice than to commit injustice. Why shouldn't this noble humane document by a courageous child further elucidate that testimony for us?

Scene from the movie:

Otto Frank	Joseph Schildkraut
Edith Frank	Gusti Huber
Anne	Milly Perkins
Margot	Diane Baker
Mr. Van Daan	Lou Jacobi
Mrs. Van Daan	Shelley Winters
Peter	Richard Beymer
Mr. Dussel	Ed Wynn
Mr. Kraler	Douglas Spencer
Miep	Dody Heath
Producer and Director	George Stevens

Therefore we agree with the sociologists Karl Mannheim and Robert Jungk, who believe that democratic society needs an honest, pure myth, directed toward the future of mankind, which can inspire our young people to actions of courage and sacrifice in the service of tomorrow's world.

In the nineteenth century the French sociologist Gabriel Tarde said: "Culture is imitation." The dramatic repetition serves as an historical testimony, as an existential *pro memoire*. As Jane Harrison says: "Pre-done-re-done."

From the pedagogical point of view it is relevant to explain here that education is impossible without *identification with an exemplary past, an educational ideal*. In many places and in many situations, where the faith of youth has been severely shaken, it has been re-affirmed (and what educator would underestimate the importance of this?) by confrontation with the diary and by the vision of Anne Frank as the *symbol of a child who believed in the future*. In addition, her trust in her father, Otto Frank, the only surviving member of this good family, has made him an acceptable and approachable father figure for many young people, as we see from the great number of letters addressed to him.

It is also understandable that the therapeutic function of the diary is most noticeable in Japan and Germany, where a child's expectations for the future were left behind in the ruins of a destroyed society, like the hope in Pandora's box.

Anne Frank's place in Jewish history

We have learned to see the diary as a powerful testimony for the victory of positive forces. We may also postulate here that the diary is a testimony typical of the Jews, full of faith in a better world, a faith which cannot be shaken by suffering.

Here a daughter of the most oppressed group of Jewish people, a modern Deborah, has called out for continued faith in mankind to withstand the blows of a cruel fate. With fine intuition, Anne Frank unmasks this fate as the disastrous consequence of the wicked work of man, and proposes on the other hand the *good choice,* which is the only condition for a better world. Anne repeatedly gives evidence of deep faith in her people: "Then Jews, instead of being doomed, will be held up as an example . . . and for that reason only do we have to suffer now."

Anne's faith was supported and confirmed by the deeds of charity and human solidarity by non-Jewish fellow citizens who sacrificed life and property for their Jewish brothers. In the shadow of the Wester-tower an act of cooperation and aid was carried out which has moved the whole world as a symbol of fundamental coexistence. Simple people, like Noah in the time of immorality and injustice, helped to save the honor of the human race. And we see again in Anne Frank's diary that men in need learn who their real friends are, and that the powers of evil are, ultimately, no match for good will and mutual understanding. Love is stronger than hate and death, and all the brutal methods used by the Nazis were unable to prevent a simple Jewish girl, cruelly murdered, from living on in the hearts of millions.

The dramatic action in the diary

From the preceding it follows that the diary may never change into a cult play in the sentimental sense, because its myth would then degenerate into a pseudo-myth. It may only be retold in order to put new forces into action. The simplicity of Anne's language makes the diary more moving than any play inspired by it. One can see this in the following newspaper review from Moscow, October 31, 1960:

Students of the Moscow University gave their first night performance of "The diary of Anne Frank" based on the play by Frances G. and Albert Hackett. The stage manager Ivan Solovjov, attached to the Moscow Yermolova theatre, had announced that the Russians who adapted the play, have tried to lay emphasis on the social and political aspect, yet at the same time keeping as much as possible to the original text. "All Anne's monologues are substituted by passages from her diary, a document that has a far greater power of accusation than the play," writes Solovjov.

Theater Company "Theater"
The Netherlands
Rob de Vries   Otto Frank
Martine Crefcour   Anne
Mia Goossen   Miep

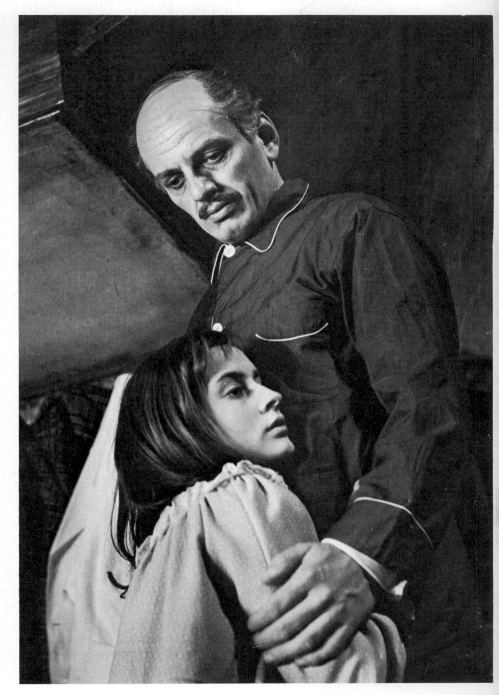

After the première in Amsterdam, November 27, 1956, Queen Juliana of the Netherlands, her husband Prince Bernhard, Rob de Vries.

This does not alter the fact that Francis Goodrich and Albert Hackett did an excellent job with the stage adaption of the diary.

From the pedagogical viewpoint we should consider the play more important than the film, because the film only reaches its audience, while the play — usually performed by young amateurs — affects its actors as well. This is apparent in the following letters, written to Otto Frank by two young American men.

'I'm a boy in High School, very much interested in drama, and this year our school is putting on the *Diary of Anne Frank.* I've got the role of Mr. Dussel, and naturally I turned to the original diary for a more complete description of Dussel. When I bought the book, I figured I should hurry and get it over with. I'd heard a lot about it, but figured it would be boring. Before I read the diary, I had my prejudice against certain minorities, and to a certain degree, against the Jewish people. I read the book in three days, and just finished it a few hours ago. I was shocked, horrified, deeply inspired, deeply moved and changed, in three short days. I've spent the last few hours meditating and thinking. I have before me one of the great books of all time. I have before me one of the great weapons against bigotry, war, and injustice the world has ever seen. I have completely changed my outlook on many things. I can honestly say, that as a direct result from reading the diary I hold no malign feelings towards any human being whatever his race, creed or colour. For not only does Anne stand for the Jews, but for any human being who suffered because of his beliefs, colour or race. For a person gets an insight into what persecution does to a man's soul, his spirit and mind. We see that a human being has certain rights, and these rights are not to be broken by other individuals. The reader gets a first hand report on the effects of war on individuals. Not a group, nation etc., but real individuals. . .'

'. . . I am writing to you because I have just completed a most memorable adventure in my lifetime. This was the production of the play "The Diary of Anne Frank," by our community theatre. . .

It was my good fortune to be named director of this play. . . When I was given the assignment, it seemed to me it would just be another play. I began at once to work on the background of the story and the first thing of course was to read the play I was to direct. I found myself very moved and it was then that I decided to look deeper into the subject.

I unearthed a "Life" magazine story about your plight and studied even further by reading Ernst Schnabel's book "Anne Frank — A Portrait in Courage." Following this, I read other stories about life in the camps — Auschwitz, Belsen, etc. It was not, of course, a very enjoyable work I found myself doing.

When I think of my own life during these times (I was born in 1932) the most terrible pangs of guilt strike me. To realize that my life was one of comfort, of freedom, of — I am ashamed to say — almost carefree existence, I shudder when I think of your experiences and those of your family.

It really is difficult to understand why I am writing to you. I know you want to forget what happened and perhaps we in the rest of the world should have enough sense to permit you this partial release from those terrible days. Yet I find myself impelled by the momentum of what Anne's story has meant to me personally. In doing the play, I soon realized I was going through more than just the motions of directing a play. I knew that I was undergoing an experience. Each night of rehearsal I saw these people — Kraler, Dussel, the Van Daan's all coming to life before me. Then, in reading about their fates, my heart was touched by what I was doing. I yearned to tell the world: Don't forget this! It must never happen again!

Again I must confess I can't fully explain this letter to you. I only know it is my hope you will realize that you are serving the conscience of the world by allowing your story to be told. More than ten thousand feet of death-camp films, more than a hundred Eichmann trials, more than anything I have ever

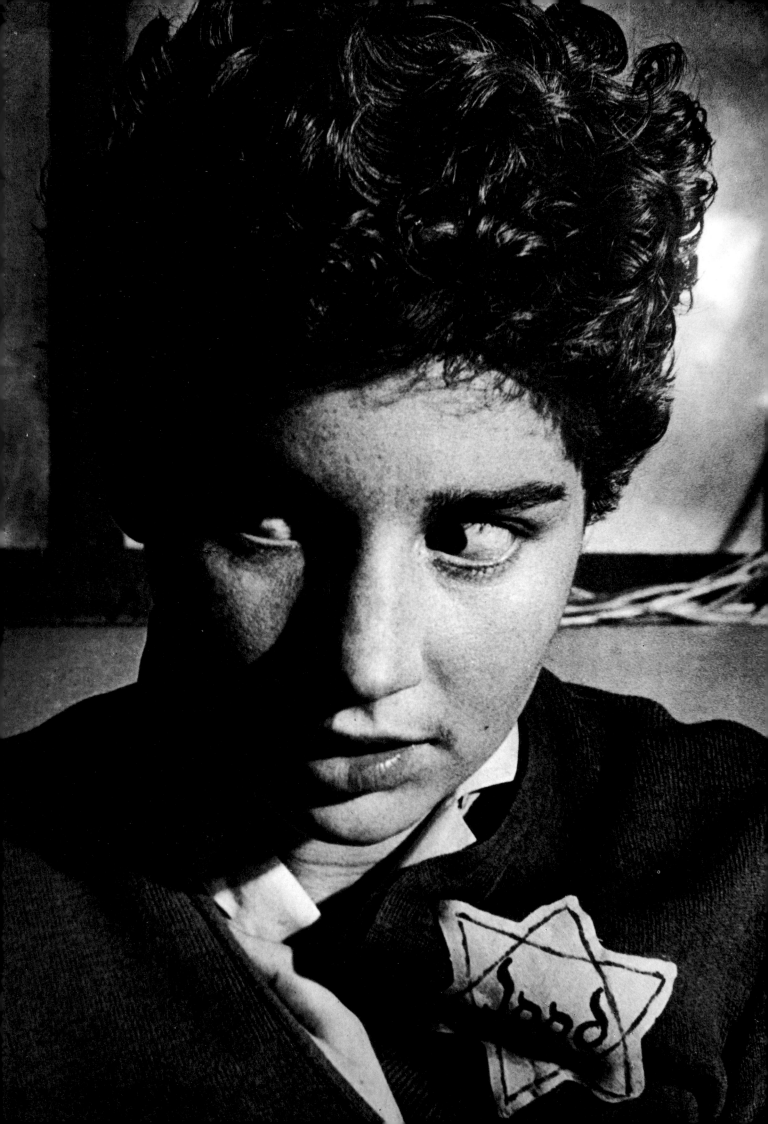

Girls who played the role of Anne

Johanna von Koczian	Berlin, West Germany
Anna Maria Guarnieri	Rome
Milly Perkins	Movie, U.S.A.
Mina Mitsui	Japan
Perlita Neilson	London
Milena Dapčević	Moscow
Ingrid Söderblom	Helsinki

Japan. Hanukkah:
"We kindle this Hanukkah light to celebrate the great and wonderful deeds wrought through the zeal with which God filled the hearts of the heroic Maccabees, two thousand years ago. They fought against indifference, against tyranny and oppression, and they restored our Temple to us. May these lights remind us that we should ever look to God, whence cometh our help. Amen."

Skin Kizo   Otto Frank

Poland. Anne and Peter:
"I know it's terrible, trying to have any faith... when people are doing such horrible things...But you know what I sometimes think? I think the world may be going through a phase, the way I was with Mother. It'll pass, maybe not for hundreds of years, but someday ... I still believe in spite of everything that people are really good at heart.

Halina Piechowska   Anne
Adam Wolànczyk   Peter

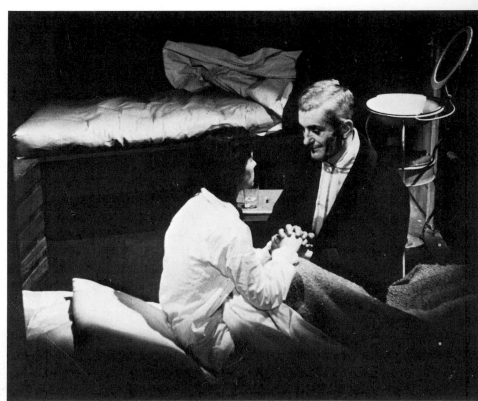

France. Anne and her Father:
"I have a nicer side, Father... a sweeter, nicer side. But I'm scared to show it. I'm afraid that people are going to laugh at me if I'm serious. So the mean Anne comes to the outside and the good Anne stays on the inside, and I keep on trying to switch them around and have the good Anne outside and the bad Anne inside and be what I'd like to be ... and might be ... if only...only..."

Pascale Audret   Anne
Michel Etcheverry   Otto Frank

44

experienced, the story of yourself and Anne and the days of the 'Secret Annex' have reminded me of what we have done; what we as human beings permitted to happen.

... My words of themselves, I am sure will not clearly express my feelings; I hope this letter will at least assure you that you have my love, my affection, my sympathy and my sincere hope that the story you have told will ring down through the years as a lesson of humanity in such a time of horror...'

The play had the greatest effect on German audiences. Young Americans could act in the play, but in Germany professional actors and actresses were generally necessary. For what German school association could have felt comfortable playing the role of German Jews on the stage? Professor Louis de Jong wrote about performances in Germany in Reader's Digest in 1957: "When the play opened in seven German cities simultaneously, no one knew how the audiences would react. The drama progressed through its eight brief scenes. No Nazis were seen on the stage, but their ominous presence made itself felt every minute. Finally, at the end, Nazi jackboots were heard storming upstairs to raid the hiding place. At the end of the epilogue only Anne's father was on the stage, a lonely old man. Quietly he told how he received news that his wife and daughters had died. Picking up Anne's slim diary, he turned back the pages to find a certain passage and, as he found it, her young, confident voice was heard, saying: *In spite of everything, I still believe that people are really good at heart.* Packed audiences received Anne Frank's tragedy in a silence heavy with remorse. In Düsseldorf people did not even go out during the intermission. "They sat in their seats as if afraid of the lights outside, ashamed to face each other," someone reported. The Düsseldorf producer, Kuno Epple, explained: "*Anne Frank* has succeeded because it enables the audience to come to grips with history, personally and without denunciation. We watch it as an indictment, in the most humble, pitiful terms, of inhumanity to fellow men. No one accuses us as Germans. We accuse ourselves." For years Germany's post-war administrators toiled to make people feel the senseless and criminal nature of the Nazi regime. On the whole they failed. *The Diary of Anne Frank* succeeded. The play has now been presented in fifty-eight cities and been seen by more than a million Germans. Leading actors have received dozens of letters. "I was a good Nazi," a typical letter read, "but I never knew what it meant until the other night."

In Japan, performances of the play became events of great importance. It was performed several times in all the large cities, and at least once in most of the smaller towns. People called 1956 and 1957 the "Anne Frank Years in Japan." The play showed the Japanese a war disaster in the order of magnitude of the bombings at Hiroshima and Nagasaki.

Clearly, the dramatization of the diary had its use everywhere in the world. Experienced as a cult drama or as a morality play, it continues to act as a catalyst for the noblest human sentiments. Its strongest effect was pedagogical where the play was performed by young people as in the Anglo-Saxon countries. In the U.S. and England, for example, the play is still performed monthly by one drama group or another, in high schools, colleges and universities. There, it functions as social drama, and deeply involves not only the leading actress, but the whole company. People feel: *we* have played a part in the drama of the diary. We are passing on the breath of the diary to our own generation, and have worked together on something with a more than transitory significance.

The Unlooseable Chain

Once as we swung among branches,
Do you remember, brother,
Our mother calling our names aloud,
High aloft, brother,
Surely she knew that strife was our portion,
For she, too, the gallant one,
Was acquainted with strife —
Sweet it was, mild, and near at hand,
The appletree odor around Jacobi,

And bitter the scent of the walnut trees.
Desk and bench were ready,
The boys learned many things:
Tongues and countries and times,
The Pythagorean precept.
One thing they were not told:
WALNUT IS USEFUL FOR
GUNSTOCKS.

Later the Plane Tree Avenue,
And we sculled our skiffs,
Serene now in the green
Darkness by Hölderlin's Tower.
Leading voices were with us:
Rachel, Susannah —
Glad to your ear, brother; to mine,
Whispering darkly of love.
Beautiful harbinger names.
And none let us guess at
THE FINAL COLLECTIVE NAME
ANNE FRANK.

But now if the quince's leaves
Still in November light glow
With holy illusions of bliss
And creature-innocence
Whose is this last
Forgotten fruit
High in the crown?
Rachel, Susannah, brother in the treetop,
Now surely the unlooseable chain
Strangles our throats:
TREE-FRUIT, FRUIT-KERNEL, CORE,
PRUSSIC ACID, AUSCHWITZ.

Albrecht Goes,
Germany

21/140

Babi Yar

No monument stands over Babi Yar.
A drop sheer as a crude gravestone.
I am afraid.
        Today I am as old in years
as all the Jewish people.
Now I seem to be
        a Jew.
Here I plod through ancient Egypt.
Here I perish crucified, on the cross,
and to this day I bear the scars of nails.
I seem to be
        Dreyfus
The Philistine
        is both informer and judge
I am behind bars.
        Beset on every side.
Hounded,
        spat on,
                slandered.
Squealing, dainty ladies
in flounced Brussels lace
stick their parasols into my face.
I seem to be then
        a young boy in Byelostok
Blood runs, spilling over the floors.
The barroom rabble-rousers
give off a stench of vodka and onion.
A boot kicks me aside, helpless.
In vain I plead with these pogrom bullies.
While they jeer and shout,
        "Beat the Yids. Save Russia!"
some grain marketeer beats up my mother.

O, my Russian people!
        I know

I seem to be Anne Frank
transparent,
        as a branch in April.
And I love.
        And have no need of phrases.
My need is that we gaze into each other.
How little we can see or smell!
We are denied the leaves,
        we are denied the sky.
Yet we can do so much — tenderly
embrace each other in a dark room.
They're coming here?
                Be not afraid. Those are the
booming sounds of spring:
        spring is coming here.
Come then to me.
        Quick, give me your lips.
Are they smashing down the door?
                No, it's the ice breaking....
The wild grasses rustle over Babi Yar.
The trees look ominous,
        like judges.
Here all things scream silently,
        and, baring my head,
slowly I feel myself
        turning gray.
And I myself
        am one massive, soundless scream
above the thousand thousand buried here.
I am
        each old man
        here shot dead.
I am
        every child
        here shot dead.
Nothing in me
        shall ever forget!
The "Internationale," let it
        thunder
when the last antisemite on earth
        is buried forever.
In my blood there is no Jewish blood.

After Reading Anne Frank's Diary

I see myself alone in a dungeon ...(Diary 11/8/43)
...and yet if I look up into the heavens, I
think that it will all come right ...(Diary 7/15/44)
Magnificent star, Mars, forever and ever
pacing in burnished bronze round the remote
unwavering watchfires of the Universe;
or vast Orion, swaying through the dark
a billion years beyond, and Pleiades
fleeing before him from Boeotia still,
yellow hair turned to starlight streaming back
back down the intervening ages — Stop. . .
Were you not shaken? Did Creation not
shudder when those two million Jews
were gased and shoveled into lime pits? When
so many eyes turned you to carrion?

I have read Anne Frank's book. She was of them.
She too, Seven Sisters, fled — but no high hand
apotheosed her or rescued her
or lightly waked her out of the nightmare.
Anne Frank is dead.
What shall account to those small broken putrefying bones
for the lost flesh full of love, the eyes
full of the panorama of a thousand stars?
Lost lost lost lost lost.

Anne Frank. Her murder be upon all
who were of humanity — such as it was —
establishing that historical precedent,
and did not die of it. Each time
we plead significance now, saying we love,
or have grasped galaxies, or have waked
out of dreamt dungeons and praise God —
each time we except her,
who was not allowed, who asked for air and got gas —
while the executioner
grinned through the double glass, I,
walking this January night, can only,
in the private astronomies of my mind,
fix some small body — not so fierce as Mars
or large as Orion among constellations
or numerous as the Pleiades —
some small star saying, It is Anne Frank,
indeed aware now
of unmitigated nightmare.

She too is dead.

Anne Frank

We lived in jails and bats' dungeons,
But the child lived in her young heart's freedom.

We danced in brothers' blood, and pain, and tears,
But the child drew Man's portrait in an account book.

Our ears were deaf, and blind the pupils of our eyes,
But the child saw the heavens and knew her own worth.

We came bawling through Amsterdam, conquerors of the world,
But the child heard the hours strike in the Prinsengracht.

We decked ourselves with medals, with banners, and with
speeches,
But the child was arrayed in shame and want and rags.

We swooned to impotence in the serfdom of our days,
But the child's slim shoulders bore the burden of love.

We were weak, we would not see when men were done to death,
But the child was stronger than Herod and the black death of
Belsen.

Anonymous
Germany

Poem on May 5th*

There are images
which one cannot bear
like that
of Hitler
I can't stand the
little moustache
behind which his throat was
like an opened grave
calling for Jews
give give give
and never were there enough
for his kingdom of the dead.

I find a picture
of this man
in a magazine
I want to write down a number
six six six
what's against it
all the names were changed
to numbers
I want to describe the features
of the Beast.

A picture
of Anne Frank
and the Annex
are only separated by two pages
from the number
I feel like swearing.

Anne Frank lives
there is resurrection
in her face
I can't take my eyes
off her hands
with which she wrote down suffering
and future.

We shall read her diary
until the Messiah comes.

G. Boogaard
The Netherlands
*Liberation Day

Later Reactions by Contemporaries

For my children that they may know.

I have followed the trail of Anne Frank. It leads out of Germany and back into Germany, for there was no escape.

It is a delicate trail, winding to schools and through dreams, across the borders of exile to the threshold of her hiding place — and at the becoming the pathway to death. It has been smudged by time and forgetfulness. In my search I followed up seventy-six persons who had known Anne and accompanied her some little distance, or had themselves gone similar ways, or who had knowingly or unknowingly crossed her path. Fifty of them were persons I found named or mentioned in Anne's diary. The names of others were given me in the course of my search or I ran across them by chance. Of these seventy-six persons, I found only forty-two. Eighteen were dead; only seven had died natural deaths. Ten others were either missing or, I was told, had left Europe. Six I was unable to find at home. But forty-two persons have told me or written down for me what they remember of Anne.

The testimony of my forty-two witnesses taken together do not make a biography for, as I have said, the child has left only a faint trail behind her. She was gracious, capricious at times, and full of ideas. She had a tender, but also a critical spirit; a special gift for feeling deeply and for fear, but also her own special kind of courage. She had intelligence, but also many blind spots; a great deal of precocity accompanied by extraordinary childishness; and a sound and infrangible moral sense even in the most hopeless misery.

What was the source in this child of the power her name exerts throughout the world? Was this power, perhaps, not something within her, but something outside of and above her? It would be the task of a biography to explain both the person and this mystery.

From: "Anne Frank, Spur eines kindes. Ein Bericht von Ernst Schnabel."

One of the witnesses said: I "was sent to the infirmary barracks, and there I saw Mrs. Frank again. I lay down beside her. She was very weak and no longer eating, scarcely in her right mind. Whatever food she was given she collected under her blanket, saying that she was saving it for her husband, because he needed it — and then the bread spoiled under the blanket.

"I don't know whether she was so weakened because she was starving, or whether she had stopped eating because she was too weak to eat. There was no longer any way of telling. I watched her die, without a murmur, and I thought: Now I will die, too. But the Polish woman doctor in the barracks said to me: 'You will pull through. You still have your face.'"

This was an exact quotation, Mrs. deWiek said, and she was still wondering what the Polish doctor had meant. She had not fathomed it, and wanted to know whether I could.

But I did not tell her that I did.

I have seen photographs of the roundups and the arrests and the shipments of prisoners, and photographs of the concentration camps. And I saw that many of the victims gave up the moment they were arrested, and lost their faces... Some of them really had faces that were no longer human... they looked like garroted angels, and no longer belonged to this world.

Mrs. deWiek says: "I don't know whether I am using the term correctly, but I might say, for example, that Anne still had her face, up to the last. Actually she seemed to me in Auschwitz even more beautiful than in Westerbork, although she now no longer had her long hair. On our arrival our heads had been shaved; they needed women's hair — for power belting and pipejoint packing in U-boats, I think. But now you could see that her beauty was wholly in her eyes, in her eyes alone, which seemed to grow bigger the thinner she became. Her gaiety had vanished, but she was still lively and sweet, and with her charm she sometimes secured things that the rest of us had long since given up hoping for..."

Bust of Anne Frank
Betsie Sturm-van den Bergh
1958. The Netherlands

54

"We were divided into groups of five for roll call, work, and distribution of food. You see, we had only one cup to each group of five. Anne was the youngest in her group, but nevertheless she was the leader of it. She also distributed the bread in the barracks, and she did it so well and fairly that there was none of the usual grumbling.

"Here is another example. We were always thirsty, so thirsty that at roll call we would stick out our tongues if it happened to be raining or snowing, and many became sick from bad water. But the thirst was worse than any sickness. And once, when I was so far gone that I almost died because there was nothing to drink, Anne suddenly came to me with a cup of coffee. To this day I don't know where she got it.

"She, too, was the one who saw to the last what was going on all around us. We had long since stopped seeing. Who bothered to look when the flames shot up into the sky from the crematories at night? Or when in the neighboring barracks they suddenly ordered,'Block closed,' and we knew that now people were being selected and gassed? It scarcely troubled us — we were beyond feelings. . . We scarcely saw and heard these things any longer. Something protected us, kept us from seeing. But Anne had no such protection, to the last. I can still see her standing at the door and looking down the camp street as a herd of naked gypsy girls was driven by, to the crematory, and Anne watched them going and cried. And she cried also when we marched past the Hungarian children who had already been waiting half a day in the rain in front of the gas chambers, because it was not yet their turn. And Anne nudged me and said:'Look, look. Their eyes. . .'

"She cried. And you cannot imagine how soon most of us came to the end of our tears. . .

"On October 30 there was another 'selection.' The block was closed again, but this time we had to wait naked on the mustering ground, and it took a long time. Then we had to file singly, one behind the other, into the barracks, and inside a searchlight was set up. There stood the doctor, and we had to step into the light. But this time we saw that he picked out a great many who were not too sick or old, and then we knew that they would escape and that the old and sick would be gassed after all.

"In front of us stood a woman who was sixty, but she said she was forty and she was allowed to go along to Belsen. Then it was my turn, and I, too, made myself ten years younger. I called out to the doctor: 'I am twenty-nine. And I have never had dysentery yet.'

"But he jerked his thumb and sent me to join the old and sick.

"Then came Mrs. Frank — and she, too, joined our group at once.

"Then it was the turn of the two girls, Anne and Margot. Even under the glare of that searchlight Anne still had her face, and she encouraged Margot, and Margot walked erect into the light. There they stood for a moment, naked and shaven-headed, and Anne looked over at us with her unclouded face, looked straight and stood straight, and then they went on. We could not see what was on the other side of the searchlight. Mrs. Frank screamed:'The children! Oh God. . .'

"Mrs. Frank died anyway, later. And my husband died too. . . Mr. van Daan was gassed. Mr. Frank saw him marching to the gas chamber. Mr. Dussel was sent back to Germany, and died in Neuengamme. Peter was taken along by the SS when they left Auschwitz in January. Mr. Frank was in the infirmary at the time, and he had tried to persuade Peter to hide in the infirmary also, but Peter did not dare.

"So they took Peter with them. They took along all who could still walk on that great trek, even the one or two hundred dwarfs from Hungary who had been in the camp for ages. The SS had kept them from being gassed because the dwarfs amused them. Now they took them along. It was cold, and the roads covered with ice. Most of them were never heard of again. Peter van Daan was among these.

Press Clipping
Vatican City, April 19, 1963 (AP)

Pope John received the father of Anne Frank today in a private audience. He was holding a copy of The Diary of Anne Frank as he welcomed them. Vatican sources quoted Pope John as saying he was happy that "the seeds planted by Anne could flower" and he hoped that her book would "become known throughout the world to promote better understanding among men."

Otto Frank gave the Pope a special edition of the stories Anne wrote while the Franks were hiding from the Nazis in Amsterdam.

21/140

THE WHITE HOUSE

WASHINGTON

September 15, 1961

Dear Mr. Secretary:

During your visit to Amsterdam, please, on my behalf, lay a memorial wreath at the Anne Frank House as an expression of the American people's enduring sympathy and support for all those who seek freedom. Of the multitude who throughout history have spoken for human dignity in times of great suffering and loss, no voice is more compelling than that of Anne Frank.

For two years, young Anne and her family concealed themselves in the secret annex of this building, which is now her memorial, to escape Nazi persecution. When finally the heavy knock came upon the door, Anne had completed, in her diary, a gift to the world that was to survive her enemies.

Her words, written as they were in the face of a monstrous tyranny, have significant meaning today as millions who read them live in the shadow of fear of another such tyranny. Anne's delight in living, her humor, her humanity, and her hope illuminate the hearts of men heavily clouded by the apparent willingness of those who seek power and domain over the souls of man to again deprive people of the right to live in peace, tolerance and freedom.

It is indeed a gift for all mankind to receive from a child growing into womanhood the greatest truth of all -- that as man rises from the brute, the kind and the hopeful and the gentle are the true makers of history.

In Anne's words "we must look into the heavens" and believe and work, so "that it will all come right, that this cruelty too will end, and that peace and tranquillity will return again."

Sincerely,

The Honorable Arthur J. Goldberg
The Secretary of Labor
Department of Labor
Washington, D. C.

27.2.64

From the guest book of the Anne Frank House:
We cannot and we must not forget what has happened. We cannot bring back to life those who have died for the sanctification of the Name of God.
We are here to do everything in our power to maintain the existence and the honor of the Jewish people.
February 27, 1964   Golda Meir

"The sanctification of the Name of God" refers to the belief that every Jewish deed which increases the prestige of Judaism in the eyes of non-Jews increases the honor of God at the same time, just as the Jewish martyrs of pogroms and persecutions died to make the name of God great among the peoples.

A song from my heart

I who was dreaming
I who was hoping,
loving a world full of flowers,
and peace...
Where are the flowers,
where is the beauty,
where is the love
between people on earth?
A song in my heart
and a dream in my world,
a simple fantasy,
a faith in my God
full of love to his children
on a peaceful earth.

Irene Oliver
Denmark

L. GAMBERINI

ANNA FRANK

REQUIEM PER ANNA FRANK

...But the meaning of this redemption is not for Jews alone. It has a message also for mankind. Anne Frank's life and death tells men that they have no right to play God. No one, whether he be a Nazi, or a communist, or a segregationist, has the right to deny life, liberty, or the opportunity for happiness to a child because of some doctrine that he holds. Perhaps there is a special danger in such doctrines in the lives of men who deny God. For a belief in God makes for humility, for charity, for a recognition of the fact that our basic rights coming from God, no man, no group, no state may take them away.

To hold this point of view in today's world takes courage. It takes courage in the South for a Jew to stand up for equal rights for the Negro and particularly for the Negro child. But how can he condemn those who refused to help Jews in Holland or Germany, or applaud those that did, if he himself lacks the courage to display the right attitude in the current color crisis? This brings home the sense of universal responsibility. Of course, the Nazis were beasts and history will never forgive them, but how about the decent Germans who did not stand up against them, how about the German Jews who did not become disturbed when they thought the Nazis were directing their assault only on the Polish Jews? How about the Western governments that summoned phony refugee conferences which only highlighted their unwillingness to let Jews in? How about Americans whose attitude toward emergency immigration was guided by bigotry rather than by Christian charity? And how about the Jews, us, who insisted upon our comforts, our luxuries, our normalcy after which we gave a limited way to the U.J.A. or to Youth Aliyah, or to any of the causes which if supported adequately might have saved many more Jews? No man is an island unto himself, that is what we have learned. And no one can free himself from some responsibility, yes, some guilt. That's what the diary of Anne Frank teaches us. It also says something else which is particularly needed today. We live in a world of mass cruelty in which the H-bomb has broken through the barriers of civilian compassion. We live in a time in which all young people are being trained to kill. We live in a world of potential horrors undreamed of by our primitive ancestors. It is desperately important that we keep pity and kindness and love alive in the world. This is exceedingly difficult in a world of mass cruelty, but is all the more necessary.

Just as Lincoln, leading his country in the bloodiest civil war could say and mean, "with malice toward none, with charity for all, let us bind up the wounds," so we, while developing the necessary strength for survival, must keep our vision directed toward the better life, the life of peace and kindness and justice. And this little girl can help us on our way. For pity, as Thomas Wolfe wrote, is a learned virtue, and we learn it best from those who maintain faith in it, even in the midst of barbaric arrogance.

Anne Frank wrote, *I want to go on living even after my death.* You will, Anne, and by rededication to what you lived and died for we will try to help you.

From an address by Rabbi Philip S. Bernstein, New York, 1958.

... Isaac Stern came to town last week for a couple of concerts. He had just finished reading Anne Frank's *Diary of a Young Girl* (which, in case you haven't read it, is the amazing record by a thirteen-year-old girl of how a Jewish family lived in hiding in Amsterdam during the German occupation). He expressed interest in seeing the house where the Frank family had hidden, and I arranged that for him, going along on the trip.

If you've read the book, with its minute details of how the family lived only to be caught by the Gestapo in the end, you'll understand what an emotional experience it was for Isaac and me to be taken through the house by someone who knew the family well and is mentioned in the book. The guide showed Isaac some pictures of the family and gave him one of Anne.

Isaac seemed disturbed by the experience, and later, practicing in his hotel room, told me he found it difficult to play that night.

That evening at the Concertgebouw, where he was playing a Beethoven concerto with the Utrecht orchestra, I saw him open his violin case while looking at Anne Frank's picture, lying next to it. In a rather depressed mood, he went out on the stage to play. The orchestra wasn't very good, but

Isaac's playing was consummate; it had a depth and a feeling I'd never heard in him before. He got a tremendous ovation. When he returned to the soloists' room, he glanced at Anne Frank's picture and muttered (I'm sure he didn't know I was listening): "That was for you."

Daniell L. Schorr, The New York Times, 1952.

. . . I have a very special need to thank you for permitting your daughter's book to be published. To me the words of your daughter Anne are unforgettable. After I read the journal, for days I could not rest. I could see it all — your daughter and her distress in her hiding place. How different she was from most children of her age. (We have five children.) Such intelligence, such gaiety and yet she was so sad and lonely and sensitive. How seriously she took every rebuke, and how much she profited from each one! How seriously she took her lessons! And always that unspeakable anxiety, the fear of discovery. Despite everything she held fast to the truth and trusted in God and in the goodness of men. How much she had to bear from betrayal and imprisonment! Unwittingly, through her journal, she made herself immortal. She deserves to have the whole world read her words. Perhaps this most moving message of hers is a foundation stone for building eternal peace. I am only a simple woman, and can only express in words how much I honor you.

West Germany, 1956

Compositions dedicated to Anne Frank

"Overture to the Martyrdom of Anne Frank."
Solomon Pimsleur, 1956.
"Requiem per Anne Frank." Sergio Chiereghin, Trieste, 1963.
"Anne Frank Oratorium" for choir and orchestra with texts from the diary. Leopoldo Gamberini, Genoa, 1963.
"A Song from My Heart. Anne Frank in Memoriam." Hugo Gyldmark, Copenhagen. Text, Irene Oliver, 1966.
"In Memoriam Anne Frank." Music, Godfrey Ridout. Text, Bruce Atteridge. Performed by the Toronto Symphony Orchestra, 1956.
"Kantata Anne Frankrol." Seelenyi-Davan and Timar Magda, Budapest. Performed by the pupils at the opening of the Anne Frank School in Budapest, 1966.

. . . As you see, my dear Mr. Frank, your daughter's book had done more to further people's understanding of the Jewish question and the suffering it has brought us than all sorts of political discussion could possibly have done. What strikes me more than anything else in this unique book is its cry for freedom and its youthful dreaming; there is so much tenderness and humane feeling in it. . .

German-Jewish immigrant, 1957, U.S.A.

Dear Anne Frank, dear Kitty,
About twenty years ago I lived through the so-called *Kristallnacht* as a young German in Berlin — perhaps not so aware of it as many an older person must have been, some of whom would like to have people believe today that they knew nothing of it at the time. For my part, I have always felt that what happened then, had taken place earlier, and what happened subsequently was a permanent stain in German history. Later, as a soldier, I witnessed the sad recurrence of that shameful time in what happened to the Jews in Galicia, in Russia, in Lithuania, and in the Warsaw ghetto. And today, dear Anne Frank, I am reading in your diary about your "underground" period in Amsterdam. In doing this, so much becomes present to me again from that time. But I must admit that when I began to read, I was skeptical whether my own daughter, who is as old now as you were then, could understand your book. Because of the sympathetic interest that the book so powerfully arouses, however, I now feel without reservations that she could indeed. Though my daughter is not yet as mature as you were at that time, she does have the very same youthful spiritedness. And life in a partitioned city like Berlin has given her some understanding and fellow-feeling. Besides, Anne, there can be no more vivid historical account presented of that not so far away time, than is given in your diary. What might you not have become, Anne, had not that tragic fate overtaken you, about which the diary itself is silent? What is to become of my daughter, who, as I hope, will be spared such a fate? Can one hope for more than that she may become a person in whose goodness people can believe? In whom the human qualities will not be so deeply buried as they were in us Germans while you were alive — and in that regard I am most grateful that we have this unique heritage from you. . .

West Germany, 1957

I saw the play based on the journal of your daughter Anne. The performance, made the strongest impression upon me. Two days later I bought a copy of the journal, and what I read shook me to the depths. I must say that I cannot rid myself, too, of a terrible sense of shame. I tell myself, here you are, a young man of twenty-four, and she is a thirteen-year-old-girl — have your ever once had such insights into life and nature? Up to this point, never. But Anne has shown me the way to an inner life; I feel spiritually related to her, and hope from the bottom of my heart that my aspiration to give genuine meaning to my life is not in vain.

West Germany, 1957

Perhaps you will be pleased to hear that the five sold out performances for young people have amounted to a deeply moving experience for all concerned. Not only have we reached a new understanding with our boys and girls, but their spontaneous sympathy and profound attentiveness make us feel that here Anne's thoughts are surely understood; we are filled with the deepest shame when we reflect that it was our own people who brought all this about . . . But you should know that young people are growing to maturity who are anxious to build a life that is not characterized by suffering and persecution. We have had many discussions with young people after the performances. They call her "our Anne" and in their essays refer to her as "our sister." In this way, Anne found a permanent homeland in their young hearts. That love, and Anne's own power to believe in the good in men, must certainly rouse up the indifferent and help them to overcome their spiritual sloth. I have the strongest hopes that that may come about.

Director of the play in one of the cities of East Germany, 1957

... I have been led to reflect, and through my reflections became convinced, that the world's troubles are epitomized in the fate of Anne Frank; every person, taken as an individual, should come to a similar realization through careful consideration of her case, and sympathetic insight into it.
West Germany, 1961

... I could not possibly tell you how much Anne has changed my life. And I am sure that there are thousands who are in the same case. For example, some Mexicans who are here as students told me that Anne's journal had simply overwhelmed people in their country. And that is a single example among many others.
Switzerland, 1961

Mr. Frank, it doesn't matter if you don't think like me politically. The most important thing is to have respect for all men and all nations, no matter what their ideas and convictions. The most important thing is international peace, the peaceful co-existence of all nations and, if possible, complete and general disarmament.
Today I saw on television some documentaries on the political situation in Katanga and the Congo. I saw a woman murdered by soldiers, and I saw her husband driven almost crazy by seeing his wife killed.
I don't believe a child can exist that doesn't feel hurt by these abuses and crimes. I believe that any honest man, in the face of these acts, must decide to fight for a better world, a world without exploitation, violence, crime, hate and abuse.
It seems incredible that at this moment these things still happen in the world. When I was a little girl I thought everything was good and all people were good, but as I grow, I begin to know the horrors of the world. It is sad, isn't it? I would like a better and a happier world for the children that I will have one day, and for all the children in the world. A world with security, where all people will have the right to an education, the right to work, the right to eat, the right to live without fear, the right to peace, justice, freedom.
A world where all people can know the truths of the Universe.
A world without lies.
A world where all men have the opportunity to develop themselves, and where governments don't shoot people, where capital punishment doesn't exist, and where all men respect each other.
Because today, sometimes, confronted with injustice, even honest men become angry and sometimes forget to respect each other, but we have to understand these things ...
You ask me in your letter if Anne's diary is well known among the youth of my country. I can tell you that here in Cuba the story of Anne Frank and her family and her diary is very famous. Almost everybody knows it, and many young people have read the diary and have seen the film based on it.
Cuba, 1963.

The diary which Anne wrote has provided me, personally, with inspiration for my own life. I truly believe that Anne deserves a very special place in the recorded history of our world. Her diary constantly reminds and prods our consciences into trying to be more thoughtful of our neighbours. Millions of people have read the diary, seen the play, read articles, and watched in theaters the unfolding of a girl's moment-by-moment thoughts and reactions... A reader or viewer could not help but be emotionally and thoughtfully stirred by Anne's great writing ... I wonder how many people, consciously or unconsciously, are more thoughtful because some time in their lives they were influenced by the writings of a teenage girl. How many civil rights workers have come forth to work for human dignity because at one time earlier in their lives they were awakened by a diary which ends in such a way as to cause one to want to act against injustice and human misunderstanding. I hope the writers of history books will remember Anne and what she has done to awaken people.
U.S.A., 1967

The Ballad to Anne Frank

Now I am sitting all alone —
on my own
By the window —
no one about.
My mind keeps flitting to the past —
through the glass.
Oh dear God please let us out!

Why did this happen —
wonder why —
mustn't cry —
Just sit quietly as a mouse
Wondering where the earth lies
and the skies.
Nowhere in this tall thin house.

Two long years have gone now —
somehow.
But so many fears that I have known
I now can share with Peter.
Sweet are all the hours on our own.

If I turn my head outside
I see
Silver raindrops hang
on the chestnut tree,
With a sky all blue
like a silent sea
And the gliding gulls
with their wings so free.

And I feel a joy
when I cast my mind
To the fields beyond
where the rivers wind.
For I know
that all who seek will find
In nature's soul a soul divine.

Friends, I am sure
will help us —
save us.
Life surely could not end this way.
I close my eyes —
I'm dancing!
prancing!
Surely it will be —
if I pray.

But if it happens
that I die —
I'll tell why
in my diary
leaf by leaf.
And when they read it
they will see —
some of me
I'll go on living
after my death.

Bertha Klug, England

... During the six-year period from 1956 to 1962, my three colleagues and I introduced many tens of thousands of schoolchildren from the age of eleven on up — in keeping with the directive of the ministry of education — to dramatizations of Anne Frank's journal, in great theaters that held a thousand spectators and were filled to the rafters, in gymnasiums and school lecture halls, in tiny village movie houses, and in high schools. I can testify to the deep impression that the story of Anne Frank made upon the schoolchildren in Bohemia, Moravia, and Slovakia, and what was their general response to the fate of the Jewish people as a whole — how for days and weeks on end, prompted by their teachers, and spontaneously, too, discussions took place about what they had seen and heard; I still have dozens of reports from school principals and teachers, and also from children and mature students, from which it appears that Anne Frank's story moved them most powerfully — and more to the point, had a most powerful aftereffect. I can still see the fourteen-year-olds quickly and surreptitiously wiping away their tears, probably to escape being ridiculed by their school fellows. I remember the eighteen-year-old apprentices from a machine works who burst into the small lecture hall in Boskowitz in Moravia like an unruly mob, jesting and skylarking, and then sat in tense silence from the first words of the play to the final scene.

I could say the same sort of thing about my experiences in East Germany during the years 1966 to 1968 where, as a member of the Kleist Theater in Frankfurt am Oder, I performed for local schoolchildren — this time, in a German translation of my own. It would certainly be a good thing today if at least some little spark remained in the hearts of the young people there from their having been exposed to the story of Anne Frank. That such was the case in Czechoslovakia, that the schoolchildren of that country found the right answer to the question, "What does Anne Frank's name signify to you?" is something that recent events in my native land seem to me to have established.

A refugee actor who left Czechoslovakia for West Germany after the events of August, 1968
Anne Frank Village, Wuppertal.

The Anne Frank Village

Henri van Praag

Dominique Pire, a Dominican priest, won the Nobel Prize for peace in 1958. He died suddenly in 1969, after a life devoted to the service of humanity.

Early in 1949, a colonel in the United Nations Relief and Rehabilitation Administration spoke to Father Pire at length about the refugee problem. A man always concerned with the needy, Father Pire was deeply moved by the plight of the refugees and in 1950 began his work on their behalf. In four years' time he had set up four homes in Belgium for elderly refugees. There they were housed, clothed, fed and given medical care for their remaining years. Out of the organization for aid to displaced persons he founded in 1950, came an international organization, based on Father Pire's plan for a "Europe du Coeur," which would establish other refugee villages.

In accepting the Nobel Prize, Father Pire said: "I look forward to using one half of the sum of the Nobel Prize for peace which I have just received for a Fridtjof Nansen Village in the area of Brussels, and the other half for the foundation of an Anne Frank Village." He had already set up the Albert Schweitzer Village and later built the Mahatma Gandhi Center near Huy (later called the Université de la Paix) for young people, as well as Peace Island in Pakistan.

When the Anne Frank Village was under construction, he wrote this letter to Anne's father: Dear Mr. Frank,

I was very pleased to receive your letter. What can I say about Anne, after thousands have spoken about her to you? I read the story of her life a year ago, and decided that one of my villages would be named for her. The two previous villages, the Fridtjof Nansen and the Albert Schweitzer, also bear great names. . .

Thank you for your gift, which will be converted into bricks for the Anne Frank Village. For months now, Anne's picture has been hanging on the wall of my little office. In her I see all who have suffered and are suffering. Her courage has been a source of inspiration to me.

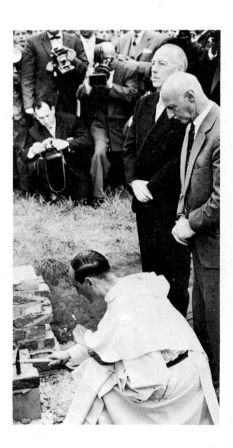

Father Pire and Otto Frank laying the first stone of the Anne Frank village at Wuppertal.

Father Pire in his study

63

Unpublished Writings
of Anne Frank

The following stories have not been published before. While not of great literary value, they are examples of powers of observation, and sometimes of surprising reportage.

Wall of Anne's Room

In the middle a photograph of the present Queen of England.

View from the Annex

THE NIGHT WATCHMAN'S FAMILY

Winter and summer the night watchman's family ignores the blackout rules. Watching them, it seems just like peacetime again, when the lights burned cheerfully in all the houses and families gathered around their tables for dinner or tea.

The night watchman's family appears to be unaffected by war or by peace. At least one can see Pa, Ma, son and daughter every evening through the brightly lit window, sitting around the table. Ma refuses to notice the war. She doesn't make imitation gravy, and would rather not eat any either, and she doesn't use substitutions for tea, but drinks a peppermint infusion instead. And when the shooting starts, she has a very effective remedy for the noise. She sits in the shower and plays her loudest jazz music on the record player. If the neighbors complain, she takes them something nice to eat the next day as a peace offering.

The lady on the third floor, whose daughter is engaged to Ma's son, gets a big, thick pancake, and Mrs. Steen, the neighbor on the right, is given a half ounce of sugar.

The dentist who lives on the second floor in the back, for whom her youngest daughter works as an assistant, isn't forgotten either, but Pa doesn't like this one, because he has to offer him three cigarettes after every shooting session.

Pa and Ma are alone during the day and spend their time caring with loving devotion for their five fat rabbits. The rabbits sleep in a cradle, with a hutch for the rain, and a dish serves as their dining table. For the winter, the little animals have a house with windows, and beautiful roomy hutches. Carrot tops and other delicacies are part of their everyday menu.

Pa works a lot in the garden, Ma works in the house, which is spotless. Every week all the windows in front and in back, all the rugs, and the kitchen inventory, are done side by side with the big charwoman who has worked there for years.

Pa doesn't have much work anymore. He is now the night watchman for the big business office upstairs and he need only sleep lightly enough to hear if any thieves are around.

Ma and the charwoman together used to clean the whole building, but since one daughter has finally gotten married, and the other just had her tenth baby, Ma only cleans her own part of the house.

Ma and Pa's greatest pleasure is a visit from the grandchildren. Their happy voices ring through the garden: "Grandpa, Grandma, come and look, the rabbits are so funny!" And Grandpa and Grandma run to see, since they believe that grandchildren have to be spoiled.

Grandchildren are not like own children, who are raised with a firm hand. Grandpa is very busy making a canoe for his oldest granddaughter. I wish I had a grandpa like that.

RENTING THE ROOM

Friday, October 15, 1943

The table of contents states: More or less adapted from the Merwedeplein version

We had a hard time swallowing our pride when we decided to rent our big back room, for which of us had ever had a stranger, a paying guest, in the house?

But when need arises and renting becomes a cold necessity, one must be able to get over one's pride and a lot of other things as well. And that's just what we did. The big bedroom was cleared out and refurnished with some old furniture we weren't using, but it really wasn't enough for a fashionable bed-sitting room. So my father went out, dug around at auctions and public sales, and came home one day with one thing and the next day with another. In three weeks we did have a pretty wastepaper basket and a cute little tea table, but the room still lacked two armchairs and a decent chest of drawers.

My father set off to look again and this time as a special treat he took me along. At the auction we sat on long wooden benches beside some men who looked as if they'd done nothing all their lives but buy and some other very shady-looking characters, and waited, waited, waited.

We might just as well have waited until the next day, because on that day they only auctioned off porcelain! We turned away in disappointment. The next day we had better luck, and my father picked up a really beautiful oak chest and two leather club chairs.

To celebrate the things we had bought, and the new tenant we hoped would arrive soon, we treated ourselves to tea and cake and went back home in high spirits. But the next day when the chairs and chest were delivered and set up in the room, my mother discovered strange little holes in the chest. My father had a look and, sure enough, the chest was full of worms! They never mention things like that in the auction catalog, nor can you see them in the dark of the auction hall. We examined the chairs as well, and found the little animals had left their holes there too. We called the auction hall and asked them to pick up the things as soon as possible. They did, and my mother sighed with relief when that furniture was gone for good. My father sighed too, but not for the same reasons. He was thinking of the money he had lost.

The problem was solved a few days later when my father ran into an acquaintance who had some extra furniture at home that he was willing to lend us until we found something better.

We sat down and made up an advertisement for the window of the corner bookstore, for which we were willing to pay for one week. Very soon people came to look at the room. First came an elderly gentleman who was looking for a room for his bachelor son. Terms were almost arranged when suddenly the son began to speak, and he sounded so nutty that my mother had serious doubts about his sanity. That they were not unfounded we discovered when the old gentleman timidly told us that his son was a bit "different." My mother couldn't get the two of them out the door fast enough.

Many people came and went, until a small, fat, middle-aged gentleman presented himself. He was willing to pay, and had few requirements. He was immediately accepted. This man was really more fun than trouble for us. Every Sunday he brought chocolate for the children and cigarettes for the grown-ups, and several times he took us all to the movies. After a year and a half, he went to live with his mother and sister. He told us later when he came for a visit that he'd never had such fun as when he'd lived with us.

Again we put an advertisement in the bookstore window, and again all sorts of people came to see the room. Among these was one fairly young lady, with a hat like those they wear in the Salvation Army. We immediately christened her "Salvation Army Josephine." My parents agreed to take her, but she wasn't nearly as nice a guest as the fat little man had been. She was horribly messy, threw her belongings everywhere, and she had a fiancé who was often drunk, and not so pleasant to have around. One night, for example, we were startled out of our sleep by the sound of the doorbell. My father went to have a look and there was this

fellow, dead drunk, staring at him. The man began slapping my father on the shoulder, saying over and over, "We're good friends!" Wham! the door was slammed in his face!

When war broke out in May, 1940, we gave notice to "Josephine" and rented the room to a friend who was engaged, a young man of about thirty. This fellow was actually very nice, but he was terribly spoiled. Once, during the cold winter days when we were trying not to use too much electricity, he complained bitterly that it was too cold. The heater in his room was already turned up as high as it would go, but one has to be a bit accommodating to tenants, so we gave him permission to use a small electric heater for an hour now and then. As a result, the heater was turned on "high" all day. Begging him to be more economical didn't help a bit. The electricity meter ran up staggeringly. Finally my brave mother twisted off the plug and disappeared for the rest of the day. She blamed the heater-the plug just couldn't take so much use, and the young man had to sit in the cold. Nevertheless, he stayed with us for a year and a half before he left to get married.

Again the room was empty, and my mother was about to place another advertisement when a friend talked us into taking in a divorced man who was terribly in need of a place to live. He was a tall man with glasses, about thirty-five years old, and he had an unfriendly face. He, too, was engaged, and the girl visited our house often. Just before the wedding day he had a fight with her and married someone else. At about this time we moved, and were through, I hope forever, with renting the back room!

Here are the seven or twelve characteristics of a beauty (not mine, mind you!). I'll just fill in the ones I do and do not have.

September 28, 1942 (made up myself)

1. Blue eyes, almost black hair (no)
2. Dimples in cheeks (yes)
3. Dimple in chin (yes)
4. Widow's peak on forehead (no)
5. White skin (yes)
6. Straight teeth (no)
7. Small mouth (no)
8. Curly eyelashes (no)
9. Straight nose (yes) — (up to now anyway)
10. Nice clothes (sometimes) — (I think I hardly have enough)
11. Pretty nails (sometimes)
12. Intelligence (sometimes)

THE SEVEN CHARACTERISTICS OF BEAUTY

Hier moeten de 7 of 12 schoonheden (niet van mij hoor!) komen te staan, dan kan ik invullen wat ik niet, en wat ik wel bezit.
—— 28 Sept. 1942. (zelf gemaakt

1. blauwe ogen, zwart haar. (nee.)

2. kuiltjes in de wangen (ja.)

3. kuiltje in de kin (ja.)

4. driehoek op het voorhoofd (nee.)

5. blanke huid (ja.)

6. rechte tanden (nee.)

12. intelligent (soms.)

7. kleine mond (nee.)

8. gekrulde wimpers (nee.)

9. rechte neus (ja.) {tot nu toe wel.}

10. leuke kleding (soms.) {veel te weinig naar mijn zin.}

11. mooie nagels (soms)

1941

THE POOL OF PERDITION

Don't worry. I'm really not planning to sum up a series of examples, and the only reason I chose it is because I read it yesterday in a magazine.

Now, you will wonder, in what context? And I'll tell you. "The pool of perdition" was in a magazine article about pictures of nude people in a movie which the critic thought improper. I certainly don't want to claim that he was wrong, but in general I am of the opinion that people here in Holland are horrified at the thought of uncovered flesh.

They call what prevails here prudishness, and I suppose it has its good points. On the other hand, if children are brought up to think that anything which is uncovered is improper, they will begin to wonder if the adults around them are crazy.

And I can only say that they would be right. Modesty and prudishness can go too far, and they certainly have in Holland. Just realize for a moment how paradoxical it is that as soon as someone says the word "naked," people look at him as if he were unclean.

I'm not longing for the return of "nature people," and I don't think we all should walk around in animal skins. But if we were a bit more free, a bit more natural, life would be much easier.

And now I ask, "Do you cover up the little flowers as soon as you pick them? And don't you ever talk about how shocking they look?" I don't think the differences in nature are very great, and since we people are part of nature, why should we be ashamed of the way nature has dressed us?

69

The Diary as a Challenge to Education

Henri van Praag

An old pedagogical truth is: words provoke, examples conduce. And with examples we don't only think of what the educator shows us, but of the totality of his behavior. The Swiss psychologist, C. G. Jung, has expressed this excellently: "Nur was einer wirklich ist hat heilende kraft." (Only that what one really is has the power to heal.) Not only individual deeds and pronouncements have educational value, but the whole person in all his actions. The meaning of the diary cannot be detached from the fact that this encouraging testimony originated under very difficult circumstances, from the pen of a child. This is also the key to the educational value of the diary. Every educator knows from experience that children can often explain things to each other more successfully than adults can to children. There are various reasons for this, the most important of which is that a child understands the problems of his contemporaries because they are his problems as well. And it follows that a child will learn more readily from the example of someone of his own age, who has already proven that the problem has some meaning for a child.

Then, too, there is a strong and heartwarming solidarity in the relationships between children. The fact that Anne dedicated her book to an imagined friend Kitty proves how strong her need for human contact was. And through Kitty she speaks to millions of young people, as well as to adults.

From the preceding it is clear that the diary can and does occupy a pedagogical role in various schools; in such countries as the U.S.A., England, Canada, Italy, Japan and Germany students and teachers have analyzed the diary. One teacher arranged the texts under psychological and pedagogical headings: *The Human Being, Stages of Development, That's How People Are, Is It Possible to Live Together, The Other One, The Absurdity of Existence, Abilities of Man, Morals and Philosophy of Life, Nature, Man Before God*. We give here quotes from the diary which are relevant to two of these categories:

The human being:

No one must know that war still reigns incessantly within. War between desire and common sense. The latter has won up till now; yet will the former prove to be the stronger of the two? Sometimes I fear that it will and sometimes I long for it to be! (March 16, 1944)

Then suddenly the ordinary Anne slipped away and a second Anne took her place, a second Anne who is not reckless and jocular, but one who just wants to love and be gentle. (April 28, 1944)

Oh, it is difficult, always battling with one's heart and reason; in its own time each will speak, but do I know for certain that I have chosen the right time? (April 28, 1944)

I've already told you before that I have, as it were, a dual personality. One half embodies my exuberant cheerfulness, making fun of everything, my high-spiritedness, and above all the way I take everything lightly. This includes not taking offense at a flirtation, a kiss, an embrace, a dirty joke. This side is usually lying in wait and pushes away the other, which is much better, deeper and purer. (August 1, 1944)

On living with other people:

I am always making resolutions not to notice Mummy's bad example. I want to see only the good side of her and to seek in myself what I cannot find in her.... I wonder if anyone can ever succeed in making their children absolutely content. (November 7, 1942)

Oh, I'm becoming so sensible! One must apply one's reason to everything here. (October 12, 1942)

...you sometimes give people like them to eat (February 27, 1943)

It is better not to delay what has to be said (April 2, 1943)

It's extremely difficult to be on such model behavior with people you can't bear... I have to press down on myself a great deal... But to really see that I get on better by swallowing ... instead of saying ... telling everyone exactly what I think ... (let me say it at once: I compromise) ... attacked the slighter failures I detect (July 6, 1944)

If the situation were ... managing ... if we ... started the road ... it could be so quite different ... we'd remain good ... to open our friends ... and out and wipe our earlier look out for something (this was to me and) (January 22, 1944)

Reading the diary, this young one cannot help being impressed by the educational possibilities it presents.

Japanese teacher reads a letter from Anne's father to his class.

From a letter sent to parents by the Community School, Düsseldorf, at its official opening in 1957:

. . . Naturally, the school must have a name. The school administration and the teaching body, after numerous discussions, have unanimously approved the following name: THE ANNE FRANK SCHOOL.

The name of Anne Frank will serve as a reminder that oppression of any racial, religious, or political minority is to be strenuously opposed. It will remind us that one young girl, despite all the injustice she had to bear, maintained her belief in the goodness of mankind. Her name will spur us on to seek out common ground and common ties with our fellow men, and to regard them with respect. As such, it is an especially appropriate one for a Community School.

The sub-title "School of European Friendship" will serve to complement and clarify the meaning of the whole: it is intended to express our desire to establish ties that cross national boundaries, and to foment friendly relations. The word "European" has no limited territorial meaning here but is meant to emphasize the fact that an association of European peoples can serve later on as the foundation for still larger movements tending toward unification. Accordingly, we believe that in selecting this name with a special view toward the future, we have made the proper choice.

In 1962, the head of a Dutch school wrote to Otto Frank:

About a year ago I was appointed to set up a Roman Catholic school in Dordrecht (the Netherlands), in which the educational program was to be tailored to the individual development of the students. Most Catholic schools are named for a saint but, since we were not bound by this tradition, I suggested we call it the Anne Frank School. A few years ago I had read the diary and was deeply moved by it. We also know that the diary has had a profound influence on post-war young people in part because a child understands more readily the example of another child. Like the children, the parents are very much taken with this name, and we hope that you will give your approval. In addition, the name of Anne Frank for a Catholic school would serve to remind the world of the growing respect and understanding between people of all faiths.

At the opening of an Anne Frank School in Rio de Janeiro in 1961, Charles Lacerda, Governor of the State of Guanabara said: ". . . We give her name to this school which we have established in the palace of Princess Isabelle, the writer who laid the foundations of racial democracy in Brazil. We want, here, to provide an education for the people in which her example will help us to distinguish between truth and error, between real instruction and propaganda, between false realism and authentic idealism. In this school we will come to see the greatness of humanity; as she too was great and human, the little Anne Frank, beloved daughter of the Jewish people, heroine of humanity and symbol for the youth of Brazil, they will learn and shall know, through her example, that no delusion must ever become their master."

What Young People
Have Written

Ruth Hartmann wrote: . . . There is nothing frightening in it, for Anne herself
stands in the foreground and is not affected by what happens behind her. The
weeping figures on the left are right to weep over the sufferings of the world; the
monster on the right can do nothing to Anne — indeed, one may smile at such a
creature who would like to be terrifying.
The hand that grasps the wheel of fate must do what it must. The only significant
thing is one's own spirit that exalts itself above all things, without losing its
vision. . .

Symbolic Portrait
Ruth Hartmann
1959, Canada.

Anne Frank was one of those strong people who try to understand life, and who never let their faith in humanity be overwhelmed by sorrow. To the young people of Germany she became a symbol of Nazi injustice. Many of them also realized that this was a German girl, of whom Germany should have been proud, who died because of German cruelty. Anne Frank even helped them to overcome the guilt they felt by giving them faith in their own power to fight hatred and injustice.

This faith, and their desire to reach out to her, is expressed in many letters.

... I have read *The Diary of Anne Frank* and thought about it a good deal. At first everything seemed meaningless to me, but no shock is ever meaningless, and no experience is meaningless for the conduct of life. Perhaps it may be some small consolation to you to hear that Anne's words have given strength to me, a twenty-one-year-old girl, and that Anne's diary will certainly be a help to many other young people in their confusion and spiritual need. And is that not meaning enough, that Anne lived to write this book, and with it bring comfort to the troubled hearts of many young people? And in that case, the blossom has not withered.
A girl, 21, West Germany

Please accept my sincere thanks for having made this most valuable book available to readers who are unknown to you. Indeed, if other persons are moved by it as much as my friends and I have been, then one might well regard it as having a divine mission to accomplish.
When I re-read the little book and came to the afterword, I was struck once again by the frightful legacy left us by the last war.
Anne's testament is exactly suited to make us young people fully conscious of what that means, so that evil may not again prevail in so terrifying a way.
A young man, West Germany

Anne's *Diary* and Inge Scholl's *The White Rose* were the most moving experiences for me this summer, and it pains me very much to tell you so, since you have suffered so fearfully at the hands of the people I was born among.
At the time I was too young to understand what was happening in the mind and heart of Europe, and I do not know whether or not I would have been as aware of it as a few individual Germans were, had I been older. A dreadful blindness obscured men's vision then. Victimized by circumstances myself — flight from the Russians, illness — I was afraid to read books that revealed the past horrors and that took us back to that time of death. I do not know whether or not that was wrong of me. But now, perhaps, I can read them with greater understanding.
Often I find it hard to grasp that all is going on as before, that things are once more following their customary pattern under the pleasant cloak of the so-called high standard of living.
All those things that should be reproachful warnings to us, and a summon and a painful expiation, are once more deeply buried and out of sight. This is a time in which evil, frightful forces are abroad in the world. We breathe them in, and they poison us. If the power of that spirit that bears the impress of God does not work against them, we shall soon be as empty shells.
Mr. Frank, please believe that there are young people who are fully aware of the deep guilt that overwhelms the German people. My friends and I want to act in such a way that every moment bears testimony to our feelings of responsibility, and every undertaking is marked by it.
I say all this out of a conviction that we are all closely connected — just because I feel very deeply that the Jewish people have a very special fate that is unique in the world. I cannot explain it very well, but I feel the power of your people, and of their loneliness throughout the centuries.
A girl, 22, West Germany

Endless pain and sorrow are in Anne's diary, but also consolation and joy, and I pray that the Lord give me so receptive a spirit and so lively, benign, and joyous a heart.
A young man, 24, West Germany

I am not putting it properly when I say that I was shaken by the book. No, it goes deeper than that. Many books have shaken me which I later managed to forget. But this *Diary* has moved me to the depths and left a permanent impression. It has awakened an idea, an ideal, within me that must shape whatever I do in the future.
A student, West Germany

I want to tell you about the Anne Frank Young People's Group. A problem has arisen for me which I have already discussed with some members of the group, but nobody could give me the answer I need though all of them, more or less, are experiencing the same thing. It is hard to say this, but it is unfortunately true that if one talks with grown-ups, one often notices that they are either completely uninterested or else that they try to defend the past and their own conduct. Naturally, only a few openly admire their Nazi convictions, but one can discover their true meaning anyway from the words they use. Not one among them questions himself and feels responsible. . . . We have often discussed such matters at home, but nothing has ever come of it. At most, I was regarded as cheeky and badly brought up. But doesn't my duty to the group demand it, even at the risk of making myself unpopular? Or, since I am only sixteen years old, should I not act in this way, out of respect for the older people? I think I must hold myself in check, and can only feel depressed when I hear their opinions. But isn't that a cowardly surrender?

A girl, 16, West Germany

I, a German girl, should like to tell you that you can be very proud of your daughter Anne.
I was not getting along with my parents very well, and for that reason, I was very confused. Then I came upon your daughter Anne's diary. It says there, "I believe in human decency." I had forgotten all about that. Like many other girls, I keep a diary myself. But the right spirit was not yet present in my writing. I was in search of a friend, and now I have found her. Her name is Anne Frank.
Since that time, I find I can face difficulties with much greater firmness.
But I am not the only one to recognize the inner worth of that diary. I had a conversation with two boys in my class who were otherwise like strangers to me, and we talked about your daughter and her diary. Anne helped us to forget our timidity and to speak freely about life. We recognized that Anne was the best friend we had, and we hope that she can help us to overcome national differences and become, all of us, God's people.

A girl, 16, West Germany

. . . Perhaps you feel that I view the world and the people in it in too gloomy a light. No, they are not better than that. Otherwise, how could the "Third Reich" have been possible, how could they have found so many hands to carry out their unspeakable, horrifying crimes? Mankind is immature, and obeys dark impulses; but there are good men among them, shining out like lonely stars whose light streams through the centuries. And for that reason Anne's diary will always be remembered, and stand as a portent to men. It still seems inconceivable to me that she, who suffered so much herself from human perversity, could preserve her faith in human goodness and love when others hated her.
The shock I experienced in reading Anne's diary went very deep, but at last I came to believe in God. Perhaps there is a contradiction in all this, that Anne's fate should move me so painfully, for if we think that our life is a journey toward God, then I must think of those people who were four or five times as old as Anne, and yet so much farther away from the goal. And what a roundabout course I followed before I found myself! I was always in search of what I believe today, I always had it within me as an intuition, but my heart seemed as if turned to stone. Who can guess how much arrogance and hatred can be concealed within a young person?
Dear Mr. Frank, I don't know why it is that I feel I must talk to you about all this. Perhaps I put my trust in you simply because "your" world is a sound and decent one.

A girl, 24, West Germany

To Anne Frank

Somewhere
you are resting,
your small hands
holding
a broken dream.
Beasts were hunting you,
and pale
you laid
behind the hidden door,
menaced
by piercing eyes.
Chained in their silent
shadows,
stars glowing feverish
upon you.
The year passed in fog
without fruits,
without garlands,
without the rain that inwardly
turns to snow,
and the sun
was high above the streets,
an aura
pouring out its fire
upon the world
but not on you.
There you thought through
the whole of life.
You drew the threads
from a bit of cloth
and painted
crocus-colored
memory-flowers
and single narcissi
that gave off
death's perfume
ere they covered you.
From your own substance
you drew
great truth
such as only rarely
blesses
those who wander late.
You were illumined
from within,
even unto the hearkening
fear of being.
The earth a no-man's land,
mute camp
of the dying,
and you, too, submerged
in death's
grey river.
But tender and
wondrous
and always
present
are your
words.
Take our thanks.

Gisela Merwes,
West Germany

... You do not know me, I have never set eyes on you, and yet I think of you very, very often. I have been thinking about you since I read Anne's diary for the first time. I was thirteen then, and now I am eighteen. All those years I have been reading Anne's diary over and over again. I know many parts of it by heart. I don't want to say much about it, but simply tell you this frankly: I love Anne so very much. Perhaps you are thinking that I never experienced the frightful Hitler period nor suffered its consequences, so that I can scarcely imagine what life must be like when one is in hiding in a rear building. You are right — I can never really grasp such sufferings — but what Anne underwent and what she felt I can feel in the depths of my heart. But just imagine how ridiculous it is: I never wanted my parents to read Anne's diary, because I was afraid they would understand me too well. Anne — my sister! Each time that I read "my book" through to the end, I would stare uncomprehendingly at the brief notice that appears on the last page. For hours I would sit in silence, imagining what her captivity was like. I would weep, thinking about it, and always the questions assailed me: Why? Why did God permit it? Why did He not set her free? Why did He let her suffer so? For she trusted in Him. Did she not belong to His chosen people? Why is God so far from us? Why was He so far from His chosen people? Where was His power in Auschwitz? Did He not hear the cries of His children? I could not free myself from such questions, and they trouble me still. And then, recently, I found a book where at last I could read how the end came to Anne. As I read it, I felt somehow liberated. What you and your family went through is so horrifying that, as I said, I can never fully grasp it — and yet a serenity and brightness overlay those dreadful happenings, and these feelings invade me now. Anne learned something that I have not yet learned. Did she find something of God's power amid the cold, the hunger, and the filth?

Dear Mr. Frank, I don't know why I am writing to you. But when I learned your address, I could not keep from writing. I am always troubled about you, wondering how things are with you. Are you alone? Are you ill? And still another question is burning inside me: Can you forgive us Germans?

A girl, 18, West Germany

**Bust of Anne Frank
by Rose Freeman
U.S.A.**

I did not really want to touch upon those sorrowful experiences in this letter. But after reading Anne's diary and seeing the play based on it, I feel the need to speak to you about the human greatness of your daughter, Anne. By her broad understanding and her clear outlook on the road to a peaceful development of mankind, by her courageous and optimistic views on a future really worthy of human beings, she appeals to me and to all those who strive for the same goal. Young people who saw the play with me said: "That is our sister, our Anne. She tells us how to act in the future, so that such things will never happen again."

A girl, East Germany

Anne Frank Medal
Georges Simon
1964 France

I first read the Diary of Anne Frank about five years ago, but, at that time, the beauty and importance of the book didn't register with me. I recently reread it, and it so overwhelmed me that I felt compelled to write you. Perhaps my entire outlook on life has changed because of Anne's words. They certainly left an impression on me that I shall never forget. When I read the details which brought Anne's short life to an end, I cried. And I said to Him, "Thank you, God. Thank you for Anne Frank."
You must have been an intelligent and understanding father to merit such love from Anne, sir. My own father died when I was two years old. It is a sad thing to be without a father, especially if you are a boy. I am nineteen years old. I was born in 1938, the year in which Hitler prided himself on being dictator of half of Europe. It was nearly twelve years before I realized how our people had suffered and understood the terrible fate of families like yours. I abhor war and anything connected with it. When I was much younger I wanted to be a military leader, but I no longer want that. Though many years have passed, I understand your loss. I have cried for your sorrow, but I have not stopped at that. I have told others Anne's message to the world. In some way I want to show my love and appreciation for Anne, for her courage and faith and resolution, in a bitter world she didn't create. Anne means so many things to all those who read of her.
I live in a wonderful country and I am a very small part of the new modern generation which others call a "lost generation." We are not "lost." We are searching for the peace and happiness which has been lost by other generations. Of all people on earth, no matter when they lived or will live, no matter what their religion, race, color, or ancestry, I believe Anne always will stand out as the one person who really stood firm in her belief, and inspired us to emulate her loyalty.

Jewish boy, 19, U.S.A.

Whenever I hear the words "Nazi," "world war," and "concentration camps," somethings comes over me, something I could never explain. It is such uncontrollable anger and fury and disgust and antipathy, I seem to change into another person. Oh! if there was only something I could do! Sometimes in my dreams I see Anne. . . then the invasion comes and we must go into hiding. But Anne is discovered and I am not. . . She is put on a train and is driven to a place where the earth opens up and swallows her. I wake up screaming before my dream ends. Anne haunts me constantly. I hope to meet you one day in person. This would mean a great deal to me. I think that only you can help me overcome my fears. . .

Jewish girl, 15, U.S.A.

Young people in America are often bewildered by what happened in World War II. How was it possible? Many of them, especially the Jewish youth in America, feel some guilt at having been so removed from the events of the war.
In the years after the war, Anne Frank became the symbol of victory over discrimination, a problem with which the United States wrestles internally.
For many Americans, Anne Frank provides the first understanding of what really happened in Europe. Her writings engender a feeling of solidarity with other people living under the pressure of dictatorship and occupation.

She wrote the following dedication in her scrapbook of photographs, reviews, and other articles relating to Anne Frank and the performances of the play:

...To Otto Frank:

In the hope that we may someday live in a united world filled with "people who are really good at heart." A world in which no gifted young girl will ever have to write another diary like Anne's. A time of complete brotherhood, when the words, "hate," "bigotry," "persecution," "oppression," and "prejudice," will be dropped from all languages because they will have become meaningless and obsolete.

I read Anne's diary for the first time three years ago, when I was sixteen. I was deeply moved by it. There were so many implications in it for my own life, some of which I understood at that time and others I've just begun to realize.

At sixteen, I was most impressed by the plight of Anne and her people and how different their lives were from mine. No one could have been a more lax teenager than I. To say that I was a completely unproductive member of my society would be an understatement. Anne opened my eyes to the world around me. I constantly thought of how grateful she would have been to have shared all the many advantages I so flippantly accepted as my due. Three facts suddenly struck me. I was sixteen years old, Jewish, and alive! This was a miracle, and miracles are not to be taken lightly. It seemed to me that God meant Anne as a symbol, to all in my situation, of our responsibility to Him and to our fellow men. We assume that responsibility so long as we possess His most precious and holy gift, the gift of life.

Each time I reread the diary, I find new meaning in it. I am impressed by Anne's death, a death that seems so remote from her character and her life, and so much the symbol of the sickness of an age. I still believe Anne's mission to be the awakening of men's mind to the world around them. Now she stands as a symbol of the past and the present, while people throughout the world still go about with blinkers to shut out the sight of man's cruelty to man. Anne lifted the blinkers and looked with compassion on what she saw. Anne reminds us to do the same, and a small, still voice in my heart seems to say, "I can only show you the path, it is for you to follow." I shall do my best and hope that others will do the same.

Jewish girl, 19, U.S.A.

Greeting card designed for the Congress of Racial Equality
Gilbert Harris
U.S.A.

"I still believe that people are really good at heart ... if I look up into the heavens, I think that it will all come right, and that peace and tranquillity will return again."
—*from* THE DIARY OF ANNE FRANK

I do see all the terrible prejudice that is going on in this world. Even in my own country, America, many people discriminate against the Negro. Talking about this won't help, but I do want you to know that I do care and that someday I will be able to do something about the world situation. Maybe someday all war will come to an end, but world peace certainly doesn't seem possible for a long time to come.
Boy, 14, U.S.A.

I first read "The Diary of a Young Girl" three years ago, and have reread it several times since then. It is one of the books I treasure most. This intimate diary awakened in my heart a love for all mankind. I am a Protestant, and I used to be intolerant of other people, but your daughter has inspired me to work to improve the conditions of the underprivileged, especially children who are the future citizens of the world.

The stage production and film of the diary were a reminder to the world of the destruction of beauty and innocence, and the diary itself has been read and acclaimed. I believe, however, that this wonderful document is best appreciated by other young people. Adults are often unwillingly severe with children, remembering when they themselves were young, and trying to bring up their children to be better than they were, whereas children know nothing of adulthood. Parents often know what a child will do next because they remember their own childhood, but a child has no experience to help him predict the actions of the adults around him. Many of Anne's predicaments were not unique to her — young people experience them all the time — but the fact that she had a gift for self-examination and that she expressed herself so well and so honestly has endeared her to youth all over the world.
Boy, 16, U.S.A.

I am Catholic; I have never been through the hardships of war, I have always been free to worship as I please. Being white, I have never been discriminated against. Never have I had obstacles to overcome, and often this "privilege" frightens me.

But now while I am still just a fifteen-year-old girl, untried and inexperienced, I need the encouragement, the companionship of someone wiser than myself, someone who has lived through great hardship. I look to you, Mr. Frank, confidently, for the help I so desperately need.
Girl, 15, U.S.A.

I try to apply her philosophy of life to my life.

I have come to appreciate nature so much more... it gives me a chance to think. Maybe that's why I like it. Just to sit alone, with no one around, and think about all sorts of things, problems, joys, Anne, anything you can name... I have come to think more deeply. Before I used to think only about things that are either enjoyable or just concern me. Now I think about world problems, school, etc....
Girl, 15, U.S.A.

"Fear"
Child's drawing by
Pedro Morais
Portugal

"Kathy"
Child's drawing by
Marie de Campos-Miranda
Portugal

Adolescents like Anne and myself must lead the way for adults — adults who can find no beauty in their world of war and hate. For we are ahead — we are not children anymore, but not yet adults, and through our childish wisdom we will try to show the world the everlasting path of harmony and peace.

Girl, 14, U.S.A.

Until now my life has been carefree and gay. I am fifteen and going through adolescence, a difficult period of growing up. I have been faced with many problems, but have tried to maintain my equilibrium. I am torn between the me who wants to be a mature young woman and the me who wants pampering and babying affection. Adolescence is very difficult. There is so much to conquer and so much to overcome.

A girl of my age often feels alone. I have felt this way many times, even with the help I get from my wonderful parents. Now I have a different outlook on many things. I am more able to cope with my emotions and feelings. I feel I'm not alone in experiencing the joys of life and living, that there are others who enjoy nature and the beauty of their land, others who love to read and learn. I am becoming more and more the person I would like to be. I have found myself. All this would not have come about perhaps if I had not found a friend who in so many ways is like me. I am speaking of your daughter who, through her diary has helped me to understand and appreciate the things we take for granted. Anne Frank must have been a remarkable person.

Her diary made clear to me the suffering of the Jews under Hitler. I had been told about the war by my parents, but it never seemed real to me until I saw it through the eyes of a girl of my own age, and understood how she must have suffered. I wish I could have done something then, so that people would not have had to hide and imprison themselves in order to live.

If ever I must face a situation such as the one in which you lived, I only hope I will display such strength and courage as you, your family and friends did. I hope I've not offended you or brought back bad memories that you should like to forget. And if I did, I'm sorry, but I just have to tell you how Anne has helped me and how I have grown attached to her while reading her diary. I feel now that I have lost my closest friend.

Girl, 15, U.S.A.

I still have to find an answer to a most important and bothersome question — why was I born into such a safe white Protestant world? Why should I be born into a safe majority? What have I done to deserve this? Am I so much better than those of other races or religions? Why wasn't I born Negro or Jewish or perhaps an Oriental? I don't know. Do you understand it at all?

Young man, U.S.A.

I am a Christian, twenty-six years of age, in college, and I have always been taught to love the Jew. But *The Diary of a Young Girl* had made me love him more than ever. How exalting to know that "the knowledge of Jehovah shall cover the earth as waters cover the sea," and in that day your people, God's chosen, will be the nation of nations. May God hasten the day! Anne's diary has become to me a symbol of the persecution of the Jews all over the world and through all generations. And I cannot but think that in her brief life her mission and purpose in God's overall plan was fulfilled.

Young man, 26, U.S.A.

I have read your daughter's wonderful diary. It grieves me that so great a person is lost to us, but it gives me joy, too, to realize that love can exist beyond the grave. For Anne's love and tenderness has truly restored my faith and given me new hope. I am nineteen, and like Anne I write, but never hope to attain the height she has reached, not only through her diary, but in her whole attitude and being. I have searched for someone to admire and look up to, and like so many, I have found that someone in Anne. She will never be dead, sir, as long as she lives in the hearts and minds of the youth of today. I believe my generation is a good one, sir. It wants peace and understanding, and needs to clasp hands across seas and continents and countries, to stand united to face the future. Ever before us, leading us to a better way of life for all, is your daughter Anne, a shining example of truth, trust, and tenderness for us all.

Girl, 19, Canada

I have just read the last entry in Anne Frank's diary. Her story and message so sting my heart that I must write you. Her story has moved me to pick up the loose ends of my life. Her poignant change from a carefree chatterbox to an introspective, compassionate young woman makes the fact that she was persecuted even more distressing. She knew after two years of reflection that there is a higher meaning in life. Anne, in her isolation, had time and the inclination to examine herself and the world around her, and to find her place in life. At no time did she blame others for her shortcomings. She accepted her faults as her own, and with her parents as guides, she sought to improve herself, to become the best person she could be. Anne began to know herself and found harmony with life; how I envy her perseverance and love. How I love her for giving me the earnestness to question my existence and my own behavior. Anne has taken me beyond the frontier of fear to curiosity, the step before self-knowledge, and this, however painful at the outset, leads to discovery. Life is the passage along which we find ourselves.

Boy, 16, Canada

I am not Jewish, but a Christian Protestant.
Strangely enough, though, I often feel Jewish. Anne taught me to love Jews so much, and to feel so much like one of her people, that even when I think of the cruelty of Hitler, I remember Anne's unbelievable tolerance, and I feel I must follow her example.

Girl, 14, Canada

I first read Anne's diary when I was fifteen. I am now nineteen and of all the books in the world I cherish her diary most. Although she is not a philosopher, a Nobel prize winner, or a great contemporary thinker, she has influenced me as no one else could. I feel strongly that the diary has become a part of me. It has made me aware of myself. I now realize my shortcomings, my needs, my longings. I am not afraid anymore. And, like Anne, I want to do things with great force, great determination.
Strong willed — yes. But a problem child? Not really. Anne's greatest gift was that she was herself. Her love, hate, and fear always bore the individual mark of the little Anne who was so full of love and life.

Girl, 19, Philippines

My library is made up of the books I especially love and wish to own, but Anne's little collection of letters is prized above all, perhaps because, as I am only nineteen years of age, I can still feel what she has written with so much depth.

My meeting with Anne came about when I was looking through the new titles at the bookshop. The cover was striking, and the introductory notes sounded very interesting, so I bought it, little realizing how rich in humanity it was. The book was so stirring that I could not put it down and, when I had finished reading it, I felt a genuine sense of grief. At the time, I felt unable to show my appreciation, and it was only after further readings that I decided to try to find out more about the people and events of the war. Therefore, I hope you will pardon my writing to you in such a manner as this. It is midsummer here, and I am sitting upstairs with Anne's diary beside me. As I look out on the beach and surf with people swimming and sunbathing, I can't help thinking how incongruous it all is. Although I was only a child, I still remember clearly the years 1944 and 1945, and only wish I'd had the ability to realize what was happening then; it makes me feel ashamed to think we never knew real war or want in this country, while so many were suffering in Europe. Only the echoes reached us and it is hard to comprehend the actions that were revealed to us after the war. Now I am older, I am better able to grasp the meaning of what you, your family and friends went through during those years.

Girl, 19, Australia

I read your daughter's diary with admiration. It is the most important book I have ever read. We know the cruelty of war and will never forget it. It saddens us to think of the Korean war or of the war in French Indochina. The world is so unstable. Young men and women of all nations must work for peace, and never allow war again.

Young man, 20, Japan

Perhaps, you will be troubled to understand the meaning of my sudden letter. But, "You are the best friend of mine" with your Anne since last year. One day, after passing the whole night without sleeping on account of reading "Anne's Journal," I recognized, for the first time, your Anne as my friend and with daybreak, your Anne consisted in my blood.

I really found "My Friend" I sought for a long time. To me who was in despair and annihilation, Anne gave the fresh water. To me who was too hasty to seek the truth, Anne made clear its great nature.

Mr. Frank, at that time, at just that time when "Anne's Journal" was written, my country Japan was going on against peace through militarism and nationalism, as Germany, as a wolf. But soon the wolf's dream was broken. Defeat and poor living felt proper with us. Thereafter twelve years passed... and all has changed to what it is today. Peace has come and militarism has been buried. Now I can live in that.

True Japan has appeared. As your country Israel, Japan is going to begin again.

You and Anne had put up resistance against an enemy of mankind, as a father, as a girl.

Whenever I think that you had to live in fear and suffer the loss of your family, I cannot but grieve for the sin of Japan.

Please, forgive us Japan! and shake hands with Japan!

Mr. Frank, but the world is going to commit a crime again. Must Anne suffer again?

As there were two Annes, there are two worlds.

And as the true Anne was distressed, the true world is fighting.

But your Anne, she taught it to me.

And this letter is to thank you for that.

Boy, 16, Japan

Japanese children seem to associate Anne's story with Hiroshima and Nagasaki. Here too, innocent children died in a cruel war. Anne Frank has become a symbol of their hope for a new world.

Reading the book, I felt as if I were Kitty and heard Anne's pleas, felt her delight, distress, and love. I shared the life of a beautiful young soul, and now I feel great sorrow at the death of a girl who had such talent, and the eyes to find the truth of life.

No person is responsible for her death; the fault lies with all mankind for allowing war. Though she suffered the war, she believed in humanity. It makes us believe in our conscience. Her diary gives young people the courage to make a new and better world. We must keep peace, however difficult it may be.

I thank you for publishing you daughter's diary. The Japanese title is "Hikari Honokani," or "Dawn's First Faint Light."

Student, Japan

Many girls in Japan were deeply moved by Anne's diary.

I want to work for world peace. I think international correspondence helps people to understand one another, so I am in correspondence with a foreign girl. My elder sister is in correspondence with a German boy, and my friends are in correspondence with foreign girls and boys. I hope that more grown-ups and children in the world will read Anne's diary, because I think the book will help to make the world peaceful.

Girl, 14, Japan

We who read her diary yearn for world peace. I, too, experienced the pain of the Second World War although I was little. Anne showed us the evil of war, and she is the symbol of peace. I am now a student in high school, and hope to work for peace.

Girl, 17, Japan

I am a fifteen year old girl and I was greatly impressed by the diary of Anne Frank. I have learned more from it than I ever learned at school. I have learned the following things:

1. We must not have war.
2. We must never lie.
3. We must not lose hope.

It is very strange that though people can be friends and live together in peace, nations cannot. As I was born in the middle of the war, 1944, I had no idea how severe the war was until I read your daughter's book.

I would like you to see a passage written by a little boy who died from the effects of radiation:

"Why do we have war?
Why don't we stop?
The things we haven't got can be sent from America.
The things they haven't got in the Philippines can
be sent from Japan.
Then we shall have only one world!"

Girl, 15, Japan

I have read your daughter's diary several times. Anne was about the same age as I, and that made me feel even closer to her. I'm sorry the Jews were so unjustly persecuted. It was only because Anne was a Jew that she was forced into hiding and for that reason alone she was killed. Oh, why was it necessary for her to suffer because she was a Jew? Why must there be a racial discrimination? Even in America, the land of freedom, white people discriminate against Negroes. What do you think about this?

I hope people everywhere will read Anne's diary, and that they will realize the horrors of war and avoid making the same mistake again.

Girl, 15, Japan.

... Just recently I finished reading the diary of Anne Frank. About her I simply say, Anne Frank is *not* dead. She lives in the hearts of all people. I wept as I finished her diary with the entry for August 1, 1944. I will always remember this wonderful work of art created by a fourteen-year-old. Anne Frank will stand as a symbol to the people of this world for ages to come. She was the messenger of God for world peace and harmony.

Boy, 17 years old, India

We are the pioneers of the Ukrainean Settlement Beliki. You had a marvelous daughter. She died but you should take pride in her. Her diary won the hearts of many people who did not see the war or understand the fascists. We are full of sorrow that your daughter Anne was killed, and we bend our heads in her memory. We beg you to describe shortly in your own hand all that happened during the war and, please, do answer our letter. We hope that you will correspond with us. We wish you good health, and may the memory of your daughter live within the people.

Pioneers, Soviet Union

We should like to express to you our admiration and affection for Anne. We should like to tell you that her sacrifice has not been in vain, but has taught and will always teach an important lesson: for Anne was an adolescent, as we are, and she had the problems that we have and the same concerns; she had no experience of life, and yet she had to meet and surmount enormous problems. Because of her firm character, her kindness, and most especially because of her great faith, she managed to deal with them more successfully than adult, experienced persons might have done. Her sincerity is an example for us, and her sufferings teach us goodness, love, and brotherhood. We understand that love should not be directed to a certain number of persons only, but should extend to all men, of whatever race and whatever country; for that is God's first great commandment, a commandment that your daughter so deeply understood and was able to embody in her life.

High-school pupils, Italy

Dear Pim,
I have written a short poem to Anne, and I would like you to read it:

For Anne
I love you with all my strength.
I love you and I never can tell you.
I love you and everyone must know it.
I love you as a flower,
as an evening star,
as the sea,
as a river,
as life,
forever, dear one,
forever,
because you are like me.

Girl, Italy

I am a young Italian who has lived in Rome for a long time. I was not yet born during the last world war, but from reading your daughter's famous diary, and through information about the Jewish people that my parents have given me, I have managed to understand the degree of mental aberration that the German people reached in their persecution of the Jews. I hope that this letter does not re-open a most painful wound, but permit me to express my deep admiration for the girl who was able to sow love in a time of hatred — Anne Frank. She is gone, but her diary remains as a universal testament to her purity of spirit. For that reason, rather than because of the book's style, your daughter is a great writer to me and to millions of other young men of every nation — one who has given us an unforgettable message that is capable of making our souls noble, good, and kind.

A young man, 21, Italy

In almost every respect, life is much easier for me than it was for Anne when she wrote her diary. And yet, I am often so confused that I do not know which way to turn. Anne's diary helps me so much at such times. I turn again and again to the phrases that teach me how to carry on. I am young, and I should like to give meaning to my life. Since I cannot thank your daughter, I thank you for allowing her book to be published.

A girl, 16. Switzerland

I am a girl of thirteen, and since reading Anne's diary, I have often thought about you all. While I was reading the book, I felt all along that I was reading about a friend who thought and spoke just like me... When I came to the end, I lay down and sobbed, because I knew that I had lost a very dear friend. I so much wish that I had known her. I know that if she had lived, her thoughts and her vivid personality would have stirred the whole world.

A girl, 13, England

After I had read Anne's diary several times, first just for relaxation (which it wasn't at all), later as a valuable and beautiful experience, and especially after I had seen the movie "The Annex" which showed all her misery in detail, I really realized how often Anne must have felt closed in and how often she must have wanted to get away and how she sometimes must have wanted to make her diary a scream of pure anger. You see, I actually thought I was the only girl on earth with so many personal problems. I never noticed anything troubling my girl friends (with one I sometimes have deeper conversations, but never about really personal things).
When I understood Anne's moods, feelings and thoughts, I noticed more how everything agreed with what I felt and thought. Anne became a kind of spiritual friend to whom you could tell everything because you always knew that she shared your feelings. Oh, if you knew how jealous I have been of Anne, of her love for Peter, who gave her love in return! I believe that boys of today don't know how to be sweet, sensitive or serious, or if they do know how, they certainly hide it.

Girl, 14 years old, Holland

I especially noticed that Anne always talks about nature and derives comfort from it. Her advice for happiness is to look at nature. Her mother believed that you should always think about unhappiness. And I believe that you should think about both. Whenever I have something to be happy about, I ask myself if I realize it fully enough, because there is so much unhappiness around me, and then I am even more thankful than before. But if I experience something unhappy, I also think about nature and about all God's good gifts. Of course, this is all personal...

Girl, 22 years old, Holland

I am one of the two Leo Baeck students who were chosen to get the prize in your daughter's name this year. It was the most important moment in my life. It's hard to express my feelings in words, but it was a great honor for me. I have always admired Anne's personality and character, and she will be my guide in the future. She symbolizes the fate and the courage of the Jews and will be forever among the great people in history.

Girl, 15 years old, Israel

Once more my family had the honor of my receiving the Anne Frank prize, after my sister received it a few years ago. It is a great happiness for me, for my school and my parents, for I feel that the course that my life, my education, and my aims have taken is suitable to the personality and the memory of Anne Frank. I wish that by following in her way I shall be able to serve the progress of mankind and the immortal ideal of humanism.

Girl, 15 years old, Israel

Anne Frank and Post-War German Youth

Henri van Praag

An important problem the life of Anne Frank raises in the land of her birth is that of reintegrating into the nation a personality which was banished during a fatal period in its history.

Every German boy or girl who is moved by Anne's story must accept the painful truth that this heroine was expelled by her own people and sacrificed to a political delusion. Furthermore, the fact that their own parents or other members of their family were passively or actively responsible for her suffering often comes as an overwhelming and horrifying realization.

To a certain extent it has become customary to speak about German feelings of guilt and attempts toward reconciliation with the Jews, as if this does not go beyond cheap sentiment. Undoubtedly, many people feel this guilt but it would be much worse if the German people were fully willing to forget 'their complicity in the persecution of the Jews. It is unjust, however, to charge all of Germany's actions since the Second World War against guilt feelings, as if a genuine concern for humanity and justice did not exist. The child Anne Frank has made a tremendous impression on the imagination of the German people. It is painful to hear of the persecution of an adult but the persecution of a child is particularly heartbreaking.

Anne Frank is one of the millions of children who have been destroyed by war. She was a victim of the violence of war politics and persecution.

It is difficult to realize that in the midst of this chaos, while understanding that she would perhaps be crushed by it, Anne maintained her faith in the good intentions of her fellow human beings. To the Germans, who were actually responsible for her death, this realization must be almost unbearable.

It is remarkable, that present-day German adults who are of the same generation as the young Anne feel themselves equally guilty, although they were children at the time. Anne personifies for them *all* children who are destroyed by violence — in the Middle East, in Biafra, in Vietnam, and elsewhere in the world.

That Germans have tried at last to make a place for Anne in the country of her birth is completely understandable and commendable. One cannot change the past for a better past, but one can hope to create a better future.

The diary has found many readers in the German-speaking world and the performance of the play based on it has probably nowhere else made such a deep impression. The reactions in Germany and Austria are many and varied. In Vienna, money was collected for an Anne Frank Forest in Israel. Several Anne Frank Groups have been formed. Many schools have been named after her, and some Anne Frank Homes have been opened. A plaque has been placed on her birthplace in Frankfurt:

In this house lived Anne Frank,
Who was born June 12, 1929 in Frankfurt am Main.
She died as a victim of the National Socialistic persecutions in 1945 in the concentration camp at Bergen-Belsen.
Her life and death — our responsibility.
The youth of Frankfurt.

At Wuppertal, the Anne Frank Village for displaced persons was established by the Dominican priest Father Pire. In March, 1957, 2000 young people made a pilgrimage from Hamburg to Bergen-Belsen, to commemorate the death of Anne Frank. In 1958 the pilgrimage was repeated. German pupils regularly visit the Anne Frank House in Amsterdam.

From the letters of teachers and pupils from many schools it appears that many young people in Germany have wrestled with the personality and the ideas of Anne Frank. The lives of many of them have been considerably affected by the encounter.

A teacher wrote in 1952:

...Yes, your daughter's book teaches a powerful lesson. It is the clear, pure testimony of humanity against inhumane, of freedom against barbarous power, of the spirit against intrinsic evil. To thinking people, to people who have feelings, the persecution of the Jews is the worst of all horrors — before or since — and all of us are guilty who lived through those times. We feel the accusation always. But when I read Anne's book at last, I was overcome with grief for all that we lost through our conduct, all those annihilated hopes, expectations, accomplishments, all those chances for happiness. For it is the individual fate that most surely pierces one's heart. I have carried on many silent conversations with Anne's portrait.

Many of my pupils — I am a teacher in a large girls' high school here — have read the book, for it is in the students' library and in the teachers' library as well. We have had many discussions about it. Often the most gifted of the girls between the ages of seventeen and nineteen are prey to melancholy. For them, reading Anne's book confronts them in a way that cannot be ignored, bearing witness to the value of discipline, will-power, and spiritual seeking when faced with unfavorable circumstances, impulses, and desires.

And the book is most important to me for another reason as well. The great problem of our large public schools are the gifted students, the few fully independent, already formed young people, who consciously or unconsciously retreat from the general educational system and from the process of teaching itself. Anne's testimony serves as valuable evidence for the legitimacy of self-education, when it is accompanied by keen self-criticism and the resolve to be self-educated as well. In that way, it is not our aim to restrict young people to the accepted areas of knowledge... but to leave them free to follow their best insights on their own responsibility...

I am most happy that you decided to allow the publication of your daughter's book in Germany, too.

The following letter was written in 1967 by a Berlin schoolteacher. She taught twelve-year-olds, and used *The Diary of Anne Frank* as a text:

In the course of three and a half years of teaching, I have never had a project that I worked on with as much love and enthusiasm as this one. For the last two and a half weeks, Anne has been the central focus of our schoolwork.

Today I invited the parents to come to class; despite the fact that it was a Saturday morning, eight mothers came. The children read aloud what they had written about Anne, the Jewish people, and tolerance. The following topics were discussed by the children:

Who was Anne Frank
The girl Anne Frank
Anne's relations with her mother, her father, and her sister Margot
Anne Frank's destiny
Anne Frank's heritage
The discovery of the fugitives
Anti-Semitism in the Third Reich
Concentration camps
The house in the Prinsengracht
The Anne Frank Foundation
Our Jewish fellow-citizens
Jewish holidays
Jewish artists
Our visit to the synagogue

The children had made drawings on these themes. Naturally, one doesn't expect sublime thoughts from children of this age but their interest has been awakened, and almost all of them own a copy of the book and discuss it with their parents. One father who had at first reacted negatively ended by giving the diary to his daughter for a present. One girl who kept a diary herself said that she found in it a new stimulus to write.

After visiting the Annex in 1964, a young man wrote:

...When I entered Anne Frank's house, and in registering had to tell what country I came from, I certainly felt ashamed.

...One may possibly forgive such things, but one must not forget them; they must stand forever as a warning from the past.

When I think about my childhood, I remember that in 1941 I was about four years old. In my untroubled childhood, I could play on pleasant summer days, while at that time small children, imprisoned or in concealment, were in hideous terror, simply because they were Jewish.

I always think that had I been grown up at that time, I would surely have left Germany, because I wouldn't have cared to live there... Please don't imagine that I hate the Germans. I simply cannot bear the indifference that people in Germany show toward this whole question. Many say that it is no longer of any concern to them, or that people should let the past take care of itself...

One of this teacher's students, an eleven-year-old boy, wrote the following essay: Anne's relationship with her parents. Because Anne was very active and often gave impertinent answers, her parents sometimes complained about her. That is why her relationship with her parents was not especially good. Another reason was that Anne had an older sister who was always held up as an example, but Anne did not choose to be as sweet and quiet as Margot. In her diary we can read that she felt misunderstood because the adults only thought of her as a child, in spite of the fact that she was very mature for her age. Nevertheless she did not hold a grudge against the adults, because she had a cheerful and pleasant disposition.
Hans Ulrich Klein, 1968

Drawing by one of the students of the Anne Frank Grundschule in Berlin.

A fourteen-year-old girl wrote:

...I read Anne's dairy, and I understand her very well. She is a girl just like the rest of us, with the same problems... Her diary is most helpful to me, guiding me through problems that often seem insoluble, and she stands at my side like a true friend. In Anne I have found a friend whom I can trust completely and who understands me. She stands at my side protectingly, and gives me a helping hand when I need it most. At night I lie awake, and I can see the people who were killed in the concentration camps, and I should like to avenge those who were murdered by thousands and buried in mass graves. All empty numbers, and each one struggling with a cruel and miserable fate. I lie awake and feel almost physical pain as my heart contracts with thinking about the many Jews who suffered in Germany. And then fear seizes me. Fear of the truth — and I try to think of something else, but I can't. I am forced to think about the world that forgets so swiftly what took place fifteen years ago, and the fear lurks, threatening and sinister, ready to spring upon me again, and my throat is in a knot. Then I begin to pray, and I pray that the Jews can forgive us. But can one forgive such things? No. But time forgets, and the time has come when people look back on past time uncomprehendingly, and refuse to consider all this. But the coming generation will keep the memory of it alive...

Drawing by one of the students of the Anne Frank Grundschule, in West Berlin.

To Anne and to her murderers:

If I open the window and look out into the distance, I think of the inner court; if I go out the door, along the streets, and through the town, I think of captivity; when I feel myself free, I think of you, Anne, that you were a captive and that you are dead.

I should like to seek out your murderers, but I know that the man next to me in the streetcar is guilty, even as I am, as a whole nation is, as the whole world. Righteousness is a mere expression, atonement a word, now that twenty-four years have gone by since Bergen-Belsen, for we are all guilty.

I remember when I first heard about you. I could travel to the scene of your captivity in a comfortable boat. . . For you have become a tourist attraction, a matter for astonishment, for sympathy. . . That is our answer — and that is our guilt.

Indifference, the dust of forgetfulness, apathy — all that make us responsible for your death make us responsible for the deaths of thousands more. Thousands were hangmen, millions are now the judges. Not merely in the case of Anne Frank, for the trials go on and on. You still are living behind prison walls, still are dying in extermination camps, marked with the yellow star of our silence that again and again turns out to be the star of David.

How many more diaries must be written in the death cells before we begin to read them with our hearts, and without wallowing in a puddle of sympathy, shock, and belated awareness? When will we understand that the bookshelf is no substitute for understanding, no museum, in which fate and misery are stored away, dishonored, untouched, under the thick dust of forgetfulness? How often must you write again, "Dear Kitty?" Will anyone ever hear?

Have you not cried out often enough, through gratings and barbed-wire fences, unseen and unheard against the death struggles of complacency?

We have put aside your diary as if it were a cheap novel. We have held our ears and looked away from the camps and gas ovens. And the future — can it change? Is there an answer for Anne Frank?

Let us force our way into the world's Annexes, tear down their walls, and free all the Anne Franks from their captivity. Let us go to the slums of New York or the trenches of Vietnam. Let us turn at last to our nearest neighbor, and give this answer as if it were given to Anne Frank.

What happened twenty-four years ago is not a legend, not a swastika-stained leaf in the chronicle: "You old people, just look how you blotted our history book!" But it is the world of today. It is up to us whether or not that is also to be the shape of the future.

We are eager to hold discussions about what happened, and to pass judgment upon others. We turn aside, we shrink away — and tomorrow our children will ask, "What was it that you allowed to happen twenty-four years ago?" Our sympathy cannot help the millions of dead Jews; the question raised by Bergen-Belsen has been fully answered by the gas chambers. What remains are "the Jews of the present, the future." What remains is your question, your accusing answer to the heritage of Anne Frank.

The answer cannot be given in sermons, condolence telegrams, and essays — we must deal with it directly. Let us draw the consequences from Anne's diary and give this answer alone: A future without jails and concentration-camps.

"I believe in the goodness in people," said Anne once. That trust cannot be answered with gas chambers — that accusation cannot be set aside with words or with silence. The Prinsengracht has become a tourist attraction; Anne's diary has become a literary best-seller. Shall the corpses of Biafran children be exhibited in museums? Anne Frank is not a martyr, but one of a million victims who succeeded in crying out, for herself and for all the others, the nameless ones who disappeared into the death-cells. She cried out, "I believe in the goodness in people," and we who know that every minute, every second, she is victimized anew, what are we to answer?

. . ."I believe in the goodness in people." The words of a prisoner, a persecuted girl, a child whose childhood had been stolen. Hope, where we

In 1969, the German publishing house of Fischer Verlag set up an essay contest for German youth with the subject "What does the name Anne Frank mean to you?"
The authors of the seven best essays, five German and two Swiss boys and girls, visited Amsterdam and the Anne Frank House. One of the essays reprinted here is by a German boy, Bernd Wördehoff, and one by a Swiss girl, Ester Walti.

could expect hatred only. Trust, in the midst of disillusionment. Anne still believes in *the other,* in the human being in man.

And we who are free, independent, contented, are we not moved to doubt ourselves, and to turn over the last page in the diary?

...and finally I twist my heart round again, so that the bad is on the outside and the good is on the inside and keep on trying to find a way of becoming what I would so like to be, and what I could be, if... there weren't any other people living in the world.

Bernd Wördehoff, 14 years old
West Germany

What does the name Anne Frank mean to you?

Are Anne Frank and I really separated by twenty-five years? One hears again and again from older people, "Young people today, the things they get away with! We were different." They say that people have changed. And something *has* changed — not people, but the world. Anne could very well be a girl of today, but yet she isn't. She loved to dream, she had tender thoughts about Peter. Am I any different? Not really. And yet she was a kind of miracle. It is hard to say why. I can feel it, but I cannot express it in words.

Anne Frank is my model. Perhaps that sounds unlikely. One ought to know one's model personally. I thought so, too before I had read Anne's diary. I read so much — too much! Sometimes I simply gobble up books, but to me Anne Frank's diary is not a book like any other. Her diary introduced me to the real world. She studied and studied while she was in the Annex. Why? Because she believed in her deliverance... Since I have come to know Anne, I have come to have more faith in my own capabilities. For one should never doubt oneself, and so Anne thought, too. Perhaps you have asked yourself, why does this girl say that she knows Anne? That is impossible. But I do know Anne truly, and all through her diary. One can make a person's acquaintance through his letters; why not, then, through his diary? Anne was no angel. She had her weaknesses. For instance, why didn't she try to understand her mother better?

It would certainly have been better for both of them if she had done so. But Anne was a person of great sensitiveness. She hid her feelings behind her merry temperament. She told herself that she did not need her mother, but in her heart she longed for her mother's love. Her mother certainly did love her, but perhaps she did not show her love properly. For one shouldn't be too severe with a fifteen-year-old girl. In that respect Anne was just like us today. She had her moods, too — she says so herself in her diary. I think that her seclusion made her somewhat different, too. She had to give up so much, and she lived so much in fear. But she never complained. It seems to me that she protected herself and her nerves. That is probably why all those people who met her in the concentration camps portray her as very serious but always ready for fun, and with a strange joyfulness about her.

When others were no longer aware of their surroundings, Anne would see that some person was in need. Only very rarely could she give him whatever it was that he needed, of course, but as some of her fellow-prisoners said, her smiling face itself gave them courage. She must have been an enormously forceful person.

Many times I wish that Anne were still alive and that I could talk to her. But then she wouldn't be Anne. For only a person who lives so long in isolation, who knows fear, and lives and has her being among the horrors of war, can be so mature at so young an age; and yet she was a light-hearted girl, dreaming of love and tenderness. It seems to me as if two people lived in her one being.

Ester Walti, 16 years old,
Switzerland

In 1969, someone wrote in the guest book of the Anne Frank house:

I hope sincerely that the young people of West Germany will block the neo-
fascists' road to power.
But all, all Europeans must be on the alert!
Fascism, never again!
Shalom, Anne Frank, shalom!

Drawing by one of the students of the Anne Frank Grundschule in West Berlin.

From a letter written by the Headmistress of the Anne Frank Elementary School, Berlin, December 25, 1969:

During Brotherhood Week in March of the coming year, in memory of the death of Anne Frank we shall plant a tree in our schoolyard, which the children will have bought with their pocket money. All the classes will be present at the celebration, from the six-year-olds to the twelve-year-olds, and by their presence will help make a living thing of their school's lovely name. And in that way Anne will go on living, and her thoughts will grow in the children's hearts as the tree itself grows.

Drawing by one of the students of the Anne Frank Grundschule in West Berlin.

Anne Frank
and Japan after Hiroshima

Henri van Praag

There is a marked difference between the letters from Japan and those from America and Germany, attributable, in large part, to the traumatic effect the bombing of Hiroshima and Nagasaki had on the people of Japan. It would be surprising if that were not the case.

What is not immediately apparent, however, is that most of the Japanese who write to Otto Frank are under twenty years of age. A few are between twenty and thirty, these include teachers who read the diary in their classes, but they also belong to the younger generation. The explanation seems to be that the Japanese are extremely reserved and seldom show deep emotions. This is a characteristic they have in common with the Dutch and the Scandinavians, among whom reactions were less spontaneous.

For many young people, this is not the case. We have a number of heartfelt outpourings from Japanese schoolchildren, often from small towns. Their idealism is remarkable, as is the fact that they have gone to the trouble of expressing in English their hopes for changing the world, so that no more concentration camps will ever be built nor atom bombs exploded.

A seventeen-year-old girl wrote in 1959:

I still remember the impression Anne Frank's diary made on me three years ago. I was deeply grieved to read it. I have kept Anne's memory since then, and her spirit and strength comfort and encourage me whenever I am disappointed, troubled, or grieved. I saw the movie, and wept to think that your lives were so much harder than I could imagine. It is difficult to believe that you could have been so restricted and persecuted that you had to live in concealment for two years. I do not think I could have endured that life, yet Anne lived vigorously for two years. I think we must follow Anne's example and I am trying to live up to the example she set with her noble spirit. I wrote these words in my diary: "Though the world is unpleasant, sometimes cruel, I believe the heart of man is good."

...Anne's life was short, but the people of the world have taken her to their hearts, and will never forget her. Everyone I know, all my friends and classmates, honor and love her.

Our family also suffered in the war. We had no food, and my sister died of malnutrition in the year when Anne was writing her diary. Her life was shorter than Anne's. I was captured by the enemy, but fortunately I escaped, or I should have been killed by him. We, too, had bitter experiences in the war.

However the world situation may change, we must continue to work for brotherhood and peace, and it is my strong conviction that the sure road to peace lies in understanding the ideals and idealogies, the hopes and the dreams, the customs and culture of the people of other lands. I further believe that there is no better way to arrive at this goal than by correspondence between the people of different nations.

In 1965, seven thousand secondary school girls in Japan participated in an essay contest on the "Diary of Anne Frank," sponsored by the Japanese publisher of the diary, Bungeishunju, Ltd.

More than twenty essays appeared in print, and the authors of the four best essays visited Amsterdam and the Anne Frank House. They gave Mr. Frank the two Japanese dolls pictured above. Two of the essays are reprinted here.

My Experience with the Diary of Anne Frank

A bit of sky glimpsed through a crack of window between the curtains was all the nature permitted to Anne Frank. It was sunny outdoors but she had to be locked up inside a dark building, and to speak in whispers. It was a life of imprisonment, the thought of which makes me shudder. The Franks were persecuted because they were born Jewish. It makes me feel the terror of war and arouses in me a terrible anger toward Hitler.

Anne started her diary on her thirteenth birthday, in 1942, and continued it until she was taken away by the Nazis in 1944 at the age of fifteen. Written in the middle of the war, her diary describes everyday life in a grey stone house, with companions who bickered with one another even though they lived in constant fear of death. I, who have only known peace, would not have been able to bear the life Anne led in the Annex. Those grey two years saw her develop a splendid, mature personality. Before she and her family went into hiding, Anne was gay and chattering, an ordinary young girl. But while a fugitive from her Nazi persecutors, she became a new, thinking girl quite different from the old, light-hearted Anne.

Anne thought of her diary as a trusted friend, in whom she could confide everything. She named her friend "Kitty" and wrote her practically every day. Writing helped her to alleviate the depression which usually accompanies life in hiding, and encouraged her to examine her life and feelings. She kept nothing from her diary — her rebellious feeling against the grown-ups, her secret reproach of her mother, or her tender feelings toward Peter. She could not cry away her sorrow and resentment. Because the diary is a real document, not a fabricated story, everything written in it moves me very deeply.

It is sad to dislike one's own mother. I often think of Anne's case. One cannot always believe her mother to have been guilty, since Anne was too young to understand the feelings of grown-ups. Her mother must have had her own reasons for her behavior. But why was it that she, Anne's mother, did not try to understand the feelings of her little girl who cried every night and was so bitterly disappointed in her mother? She, too, had been a young girl. But it is not easy, I know, to experience again the feelings of childhood. It may be that God takes away from grown-ups the antenna designed to tune in children's minds. It is very sad that this state of affairs — Anne's mother not understanding her daughter and Anne herself remaining insensitive to her mother's feeling — was not straightened out by mutual love and trust.

Her parents and the Van Daans bickered constantly, without concern for Anne's sufferings. Human beings can be ugly when short of necessities, as they are in wartime. It's more important to stay alive than to remain rational. I was moved to tears to read what one woman said about Anne in the concentration camp: "Anne was the bravest and the most cheerful of all the three women in the Frank family. She was always giving something out of her own small ration to her mother and sister, and to hungry strangers."

Either the diary itself, or the film or play based on it, is familiar to people everywhere. Anne's troubled two years did not remain just the "personal tragedy" of a little girl, but have become an experience shared by the entire world.

I see a vast expanse of blue sky dotted with soft white clouds above me. These clear autumn skies of Shinshu are for me to look at in perfect freedom. I don't have to worry about anyone else's feelings, I can laugh out loud if anything amuses me, and I can sing any time I want to. These things may seem commonplace, but after reading Anne's diary, I am grateful to have such freedom.

We must all vow never to allow anyone to be treated as Anne was. We all have to take care of the world around us. This precious lesson has cost us Anne Frank.

入選

中条みち子

長野市立裾花中学校三年

窓のすき間の細長い空、カーテン越しの空、それがアンネに許された、ただ一つの自然の姿だった。太陽がさんさんと輝く昼間なのに、暗い建物の中で声を押し殺していなければならない。鉛色の箱の中にとじこめられているようなアンネ達の生活。思っただけでも寒けがする。ユダヤ人であるがゆえに迫害された

アンネ達一家——それは私達に戦争の恐ろしさ、ヒットラーに対する憤りを激しく覚えさせる。

『アンネの日記』は、一九四二年、アンネの十三歳の誕生日から一九四四年、戦争のさ中、十五歳でナチにとらわれるまでの約二年間、戦争のさ中に一少女の書いた日記である。毎日毎日が灰色の建物の中、死に直面した恐怖の中にいないながらけんかの絶えない住人。平和な今の時代に育った私では一日だってとてもがまんは出来まい。そんな中での二年間に、アンネはすばらしく成長していった。隠れ家生活にはい

『アンネの日記』は、一九四二年、アンネの十三歳の誕生日から一九四四年、戦争のさ中、十五歳でナチにとらわれるまでの約二年間、戦争のさ中に一少女の書いた日記である。毎日毎日が灰色の建物の中、死に直面した恐怖の中にいないこの日記は、彼女が大勢の友達に囲まれ、女王のように華やかにふるまっていた頃のような、軽はずみな少女ではなく、考え深い少女に育った事を物語ってくれる。

アンネは日記を心の友としてキティと名づけ、毎日のようにキティに手紙を書く。とすれば暗く投げやりになりがちな隠れ家生活

Michiko Nakajo
1965, 3rd year, High School, Japan

My Experiences with the Diary of Anne Frank

What a great thing it is for one to be able to express, without restrictions, his own feelings of love, hatred, anger, sorrow and his thoughts and opinions about things without self-deception or exaggeration. This may well be the only kind of freedom one can have. Friendless and persecuted constantly for being a Jew, Anne Frank went on writing, with her outlook and feeling intact. While reading her straightforward account of herself in her diary, I, at one stage, recalled a little incident which occurred when I was a middle school student.

It was during the third semester of my first year. We were required to hand in our diaries every day, and the teacher returned them to us with marginal comments. The practice created a sort of dialogue between teacher and pupil. It served us as a sort of safety valve, allowing us to pour out our rebellious reactions against our classmates as well as against the teachers themselves. In one of the entries I had put down my intense opinion of an incident we were all familiar with, which had upset me. I had expected an equally intense reaction from my teacher. But the following day I received this comment in the margin of my diary: "I was moved to almost tears, reading your entry for today, because I was so happy to think that if anyone in the third year should be as right-minded as you, or rather if all students were as good as you are, what a great school ours would be. It is more than one can expect at the moment. But I do hope that you will make your good self contagious."

This nice note my teacher wrote filled me with a peculiar sadness, entirely contrary to the feeling I had before I handed in my diary. I felt that my teacher was reading me like a book, leaving me nothing I could call my own. After that experience, I stopped handing in my diary, and began to withdraw into myself. By the time I became aware of it, I was developing a uniquely sensitive pride. But this acute sense of pride, is it something so unique and peculiar to me alone? I must ask you this question, Anne: Was it not your fear of exposing yourself to others that led you to confide your dearest secrets to a piece of paper? But Anne is not here to answer my question. I prefer to think, however, that Anne felt as I do, that my innermost feelings represent hers. Dominant in both of us is a sense of sadness or loneliness when we realize how difficult it is to reveal our deepest feeling, and that even if we do, others will never understand us. This is true of all human relations, I think, no matter how close. I became too much of a coward to expose my heart, and for that reason I am regarded as something of an egoist. And I have a notion that Anne is much like me.

This may sound selfish but I cannot help but feel that this diary was written by a girl called Anne on my behalf, or rather on behalf of those like me. My dear Anne, do you feel I am too self-satisfied in thinking this? We have a great deal in common — our nature and our way of thinking, and that was the greatest joy I found in reading your diary. But my sorrow is greater than my joy, for you are no more and I cannot really communicate with you, no matter how close and akin I feel to you. My desire to become your friend will forever remain only a wish.

But you have given me a friend greater than any I have known. You taught me to write. From reading your diary, I have regained my passion for recording truthful and important things. I shall indeed write, only what I write will be kept from the eyes of others.

Anne, your diary will be the source of my strength for all time.

Funiko Tonizama
1965, 2nd year, High School, Japan

入選

富沢富美子

千葉県立木更津高校二年

人間が、愛、憎しみ、怒り、悲しみ、そしてすべてのものに対する、自分の考えや思いを、自分を偽らず、誇張することなく書き出せるという事は、どんなにすばらしいことだろう。自分だけが知っていて、誰にもこだわる事のない自由は、あるいはそれだけかも知れない。真実の友を持たず、戦争の中で苦しみ、ユダヤ人であるがために痛めつけられながらも、隠れ家生活の中で自分を失うことなく、自分なりの人生観を持ち、思想を持って、アンネは書き続けた。アンネの素直な批判を読んでいて、私はふと中学時代のある出来事を想い出した。

それは、中学一年の三学期のことであった。その頃私達は、毎日日記を記入すると先生に提出していた。そうすると先生がいろいろな事を書いてくれて、いわばそれは先生と生徒との交換書簡のようなものだった。ちょうど反抗期にあった私達は、友人に対して言えない悪口も、先生への不満も、すべて感情のままに書いた。そんなある日、私はちょっとした出来事を見て、それに対する自分の気持を、それこそ思う存分に書いた。その時の私の心には、多分に先生の批評を期待する何かがあった。翌日返された日記帳には、「君の日記を読んで、私は自然と喜びの涙がでてきてどうすることもできなかった。三年生といえども、君の様に立派な心掛けの人が他にいるだろうか。全生徒が君の様であったら……。どんなにか立派な学校に発展するだろうに。今のところ残念です。どうか君の立派な

Anne Frank and the Israelian Youth of Today

M.L. Meelker — van Tijn

The state secondary school "Kol Jisraël Chaweriem" in Tel-Aviv dedicated the school year 1965-66 to the memory of Anne Frank.

All those who lived through the Second World War know that they will never forget it. But a new generation has grown up, born during or after the war, which must learn about the events of the war from reading or hearsay. There are people who have seen Auschwitz and who still can hardly imagine the nightmare world in this annihilation camp. How then can we make our children understand the enormity of the crimes commited by the Nazi government? It is essential that the entire generation born after the war should be told, but it is especially important in the case of young Jews. However difficult it is for post-war youth to really comprehend the events of the war, it is even more difficult for the Jewish youth born after the founding of the State of Israel. Their lives are certainly different from those of the young Jews who lived during the time of Exile, but the gap becomes staggering when their lives are compared with those of the Jewish children who lived in areas under Nazi occupation during World War II. The youth of Israel, unlike other Jews, no longer belong to a minority which must always be ready to suffer discrimination and persecution. They are part of a nation, a people who can and will defend themselves in their own country, with arms if necessary. Yet the very fact that they *are* Jews, and the descendants of a persecuted people, binds them to the Jews of the time of Exile, the Jews of the past and the Jews of the present. They must understand these ties, or they will no longer understand their own cultural heritage or their place in history.

It was for these reasons that the secondary school "Kol Jisraël Chaweriem" assigned six hundred of its pupils from twelve to sixteen years old to read or re-read Anne Frank's diary, and to write an essay about the book. They were given a choice of ten different topics, including "The development of Anne's personality during the time she was in hiding — natural growth or environmental conditions?" "Religion, tradition and nationalism and why these did or did not appear in those in hiding;" or "How Anne saw her father, mother and sister." The forty-six best essays were awarded a money prize which was donated to the school for this purpose by Mr. Otto Frank, Anne's father.

A drama group, made up of students from the school, gave two performances of the dramatized version of the diary. The great facility with which the young actors and actresses were able to identify themselves with the characters from the diary made a deep impression on the adult audience.

In the four best essays, many of the difficulties of explaining the war to young people are expressed. In addition, one sees the special difficulties experienced by Israeli boys and girls. For example, one fifteen-year-old boy, who writes about "Religion, tradition and nationalism, and why these did or did not appear in those in hiding," tries to understand why Anne's religious thoughts were a mixture of Christian and Jewish elements. He calls all the non-Jews Christians, and he assumes from the outset that they are in principal hostile to the Jewish people, although he does say that there were some sympathetic Christians, such as those who helped the Frank and Van Daan families while they were in the Annex. This boy is the son of Jewish parents who suffered terribly during World War II. They lost many of their relatives, including two of their children. His parents, who were not particularly religious before the war, began to live

Planting trees on the hills of Judea for the Forest of Martyrs. A section containing 10,000 trees is called the Anne Frank Forest.

Tamar Goldreich, 1961.

אַנאַ פראַנק

אָט קומט זי ווידער אָן. די אויגן לייכטן אויף די דאַרע באקן.
ס׳פאַלט ציטערדיק דער שאָטן פון די ברעמען אויף דער בלייכער הויט.
עס הילכן אָפּ די טריט פון וואַכליַיט. שטעכלדיקע דראָט. באַראַקן.
און ווידער פראָכט־וואגאָנען קייקלען זיך און קייקלען זיך אין טויט.

דער יעסטעדיקער רעגן דרייבלט קאַלעמוטנע אין די שויבן.
צערונען איז שוין דער קוואַדראַט פון זון. וואָס האָט די וואָנט באַלויכם.
די וויסטע פינצטערערניש פון נאַכט לעשט אויס די קינדערישע אויגן.
וואָס זעען ציטערדיק. ווי ס׳ווערגן צאָן־רעדער דעם לעבנס־הויך.

געסטאָפאָ. חורבות. געטאָ. צאָן־רעדער פון האָקן־קרייציישן טייוול.
אין טאָגבוך אויף דעם בוידעם דורשטיק לעכצט נאָך ליבע אַ דין קול.
און ווידער רויך און רויך און רויך. געוואָרן איז די ערד אַ הויפל
און שטייט אויף אין דער נאָכט. אז נישט פארגעסן זאָל איך זי קיינמאָל.

To Anne Frank

There she is again.
Her eyes shining
Above her hollow cheeks.
The shadow of her brows
Falls frighteningly
On her pale skin.
The steps of the guard resound,
Barbed wire, barracks.
And the freight trains
Roll back and forth in death.

The steady rain drips into the barracks,
The square of sun
that shone upon the wall
Has disappeared.
The desolate darkness of the night
Puts out the childish eyes
That see, with trembling,
How the mechanism throttles life.

Gestapo, ruins, ghetto,
The mechanism
Of the scythe-swinging devil.
In a diary in the attic
A thin voice still longs
Thirstily for love.
Smoke, smoke, and more smoke;
The world has become an ash-heap
And rises up in the night,
So that it will never be forgotten.

J. Weitschuneite
Lithuania

according to orthodox Jewish tradition afterwards, in memory of their murdered parents. "I have chosen this subject," he says, "because it seems interesting to me to examine what a Jewish girl from an assimilated family felt when the social, emotional, and economic situation of her family went through total reversal. This problem interested me because, as an Israeli from an orthodox family, I have never experienced the mental struggle which Anne had during the war years."

It is a sixteen-year-old boy who shows that it really is possible for Israeli youth to comprehend what actually was happening to the Jews in occupied Europe. His penetrating essay, full of understanding and compassion, made a deep impression on me. I have included an excerpt from the brief curriculum vitae which he, as well as the other three young authors, provided, because it is characteristic of the sensitive and intelligent young man who wrote this essay:
"I was born into a Jewish family which came to Israel shortly before the founding of the state. My first school year was spent in a religious school in Ramat-Gan, where we lived at that time. My parents, who had been members of the Chaloets Youth Movement in Exile, and who were raised with a strong community spirit, did not feel at home in the city, so we left for the kibbutz "Giwat-Chaim" in the Chefer valley. My parents did not feel that the kibbutz was the right place for us either, since the kibbutz in 1957 was no longer what it had been in 1948. I liked the children's community in the kibbutz, however, and was able to fit in excellently with the group. Before a year was over, we moved again and settled in a mosjaw. From there we moved again to the residential section "Jefat Nof" part of the development plan of Tel-Aviv, Ramat-Aviv, where we live today.

I first read Anne Frank's diary at a very early age, but at that time the atmosphere of her life seemed foreign and incomprehensible to me. As a result I remained curious, and was glad to meet this unusual personality a second time in order to be able to examine that special atmosphere.
I studied the book as thoroughly as possible, and became completely absorbed in writing about it. As a boy, it was difficult for me to put myself into the special world of a growing girl; as a child of Israel and as a person who is free in everything it was not easy for me to understand the special background of the events which took place in this book. I attempted to enter her world and to understand the events and people. The Jewish culture outlook I share with the people in the book helped me in this. I am the grandson and the greatgrandson of a well-known family of Tsadikiem (leader of a community of Hasidim), the "dynasty" of Wisnitz. In my home there is a special Hasidic atmosphere, and that is why tradition has an important place in my life.
We so often speak of the tragedies of this period in numbers: "The city of Krakov has been destroyed," "ten thousand Jews from Hungary were murdered in the gas chambers," "three million Polish Jews. .", and because of the great number, our hearts become deadened to the individual cries.
Yet it is the person we find in the cry of the girl Anne, a solitary figure who makes it easier for us to identify with what happens to her and what she feels. She brings the Annihilation before our eyes in all its terror."
This last sentence may be more romantic than strictly accurate, but nevertheless he has touched the real heart of the matter. Here lies the imperishable value in Anne's diary for all young people wherever they are in the world, and especially for the Jewish youth of today's Israel.

263
PRINSENGRACHT

MAISON "ANNA FRANK" AMSTERDAM

DEVI TUSZYNSKI MAI 1961

Rivka Manella is attracted to literature and human problems. She writes: "Through the study of various literary works we are able to get an idea of the disasters which fell upon our people during the Exile.

Because my parents also came out of Exile (from Germany and Bulgaria) the lot of my brothers, sons of my people in Exile, was something which concerned me personally. That is why I was naturally sympathetic to a book like Anne Frank's diary."

And she does indeed show understanding of the life of the Jews in the area under Nazi occupation. She understands something of the oppression and of the stifling atmosphere of the Annex, while she is also familiar with the difficulties of a young girl going through puberty. She does not consider the diary a book in the ordinary sense of the word, but the intimate conversation of a young girl with herself, a conservation in which she turns over and over not only her problems and feelings, but also the impressions of and the relationships with the people around her.

It is clear that in Rivka Manella the gap which separates the Israeli youth from a young Jewish girl in hiding has been successfully bridged.

Development of Anne's Personality During the Period in Hiding:

Anne received her diary as a gift on her thirteenth birthday. She regarded it as an invaluable treasure; a kind of friend to whom she could open her heart as she had to no living person. For her it was comfort and salvation: *I don't want to set down a series of bald facts in a diary like most people do, but I want this diary itself to be my friend, and I shall call my friend Kitty.*

Indeed Anne's personality is candidly and clearly expressed in her diary, for in it she wrote all her impressions whether external or interior, and it was a faithful mirror of her mind.

At first the reader sees Anne as an effervescent and happy child who, however, can be serious and is capable of profound thought. She had great self confidence when speaking of her admirers, and was most aggressive in her conduct towards them: *You get some who blow kisses or try to get hold of your arm, but then they are definitely knocking at the wrong door. I get off my bicycle and refuse to go farther in their company.*

Anne had a lively sense of humor, and an outgoing personality. Her considerable talent for writing is apparent in her diary, which is well ordered, sometimes amusing, and written in a clear and easy style.

When the family first went into hiding, Anne continued her free and mischievous ways and provided an element of gaiety and merriment in the house. She made an exemplary adjustment, and at once decorated her room. She was not dismayed at their new quarters and remarked smilingly: *It is like being on holiday in a very peculiar boarding house. The Secret Annex is an ideal hiding place.*

Soon life in hiding became routine, each day like the last. During the day the inmates sat in silence, lest their voices be heard in the nearby offices. The evenings were boring and uneventful.

At first, as we have said, Anne was in high spirits and, in keeping with her good nature, that in every instance she sought the amusing and the good. But the turbulent and passionate Anne was not the child to sit quietly in one place, with nothing to interest or surprise her. Life became tedious and uncomfortable: *My nerves often get the better of me. It is especially on Sundays that I feel rotten. The atmosphere is so oppressive and sleepy and as heavy as lead. You don't hear a single bird singing outside and a deadly close silence hangs everywhere, catching hold of me, as if it will drag me down deep into an underworld.*

The gloomy life in concealment upset her, this girl who loved a free life close to nature: *To look up at the sky, the clouds, the moon, and the stars makes me calm and patient.*

The impetus of growth, characteristic of puberty, called forth Anne's talents and gifts and her desire to be known. She exercised her gifts in the composition of various stories, and in writing her diary. Her desire for recognition, too, was strong. She could not bear adult criticism of her behavior, her manners and her character: *I am not going to take all these insults lying down. I'll show them that Anne Frank wasn't born yesterday. Then they'll be surprised and perhaps they'll keep their mouths shut when I let them see that I am going to start educating them.*

During puberty, the young girl fights for the recognition that she is no longer a child. Anne's fight was bitter and stubborn, because she still longed, through her insecurity and loneliness to remain a little girl. She was furious at being considered a child and denied things that were permitted to her sister Margot. And, as is natural, she began to criticize her environment and her parents, particularly her mother. Her feelings of responsibility and independence increase.

102

Thus Anne's attitude towards her mother may be understood. She frequently quarrelled with her mother and could not agree with her opinions. Anne's behaviour toward her mother was unrestrained and sometimes insolent.

Forthright and natural, she was unable to hide or disguise her feelings. In her opinion, her mother showed scant understanding for her daughter's problems — indeed, their conflicting opinions were the source of the problem. *Each day I miss having a real mother who understands me.* Sometimes Anne's treatment of her mother was extremely harsh, and in the course of time they grew away from each other, the girl permitting her mother to share none of her experiences, seizing every opportunity to stress her independence.

The adolescent seeks objects outside himself to love or to hate, or with which he can identify himself. Anne was no exception. Peter, to whom she was attracted, was just such an object: *I have a strong feeling that Peter and I are not so different as we would appear to be and I will tell you why. We both lack a mother... both wrestle with our inner feelings, we are still uncertain and we are really too sensitive to be roughly treated.* Peter did not attract her as a lover. Anne was fundamentally tender and very feminine. She felt alone and lonely in her world: *I feel as lonely as if there was a great vacuum around me.*

Menorah, donated to the Anne Frank House, Amsterdam, by Youth Aliyah on behalf of the young people of Israel.

Like any girl, she needed someone to understand her, pay her compliments, tell her she was pretty, attractive and desirable. She needed someone to fulfill her being, to understand her, and she hoped that Peter would be able to fill the role. She suffered deeply, but kept her pain to herself: *I'm boiling with rage and yet I mustn't show it. I'd like to stamp my feet, scream, give Mummy a good shaking, cry and I don't know what else.*

Anne hoped Peter would help her with her problems, and share her experiences, *I have never been used to sharing my troubles with anyone. I have clung to my mother, but now I would so love to lay my head on "his" shoulder just once and remain still.* For a time, Peter was a "tranquillizer" for Anne, when she thought of him it seemed to her that she was happy and that nothing was lacking in her life. In her relations with Peter, Anne is shown as an ardent, passionate girl: *May I, a girl, let myself go to this extent?*

There is but one answer: *I have longed so much and for so long — I am lonely — and now I have found consolation.* Anne liked to appear pretty, and to read about the glamorous lives of film stars, perhaps even to imitate them.

Bell from the Anne Frank Children's Home in the kibbutz Neoerim, Israel. The inscription "Give" is the title of a book of Anne's stories.

As time drew on, Anne was no longer content to have discovered the love between Peter and her. She began to desire something more elevated, more profound than love. Fairly mature in outlook, she sought a more spiritual intimacy, and longed to know Peter's innermost self. But he, introverted and shy, gave no outward sign of his feeling, causing Anne to draw away from him and the cooling of her enthusiasm.

Anne was unusually serious, and conceived ideas uncommonly profound for one of her age. She was extremely ambitious, aspired to an honored status, and high position: *I must work so as not to be a fool, to get on* or *I want to get on; I can't imagine that I would have to lead the same sort of life as Mummy and Mrs. Van Daan and all the women who do their work and are then forgotten.*

Good-natured, honest and forthright, Anne's happiness with Peter dimmed when she found that her sister Margot, too, was attracted to him. It was hard to bear the thought that she was stealing her sister's chance for happiness. It says much for her honesty that, denying nothing, she told her father all about her relations with Peter.

Certain characteristic features become distinguishable under the outlandish circumstances of Anne's life. In her imagination she saw her childhood friend Lies, and was stricken with remorse: *It was horrid of me to treat her as I did, and now she looked at me, oh, so helplessly, with her pale face and imploring eyes.*

She was deeply shaken whenever she thought of the fate that had overtaken her friend, and frequently prayed for her. Often she would awaken from a nightmare, in a paroxysm of fear and dread. She suffered the pain of her persecuted people, frequently dwelling on the fact of her Jewishness and questioning why her people had to suffer so unnecessarily. These thoughts attest to Anne's sensitivity and her feeling for other people in trouble. She had an honest desire to help the tormented and the suffering.

Anne's character changed greatly during the time she was in hiding. She became an independent person. She examined everything she saw and did, and gained a large measure of understanding of herself and other people. She became impartial regarding the arguments between her and her family. She considered her answers carefully, and became wiser and more sober. Where she had previously wanted admirers, she now sought friends who would be drawn to her by her character. At the age of fourteen, she already considered herself half grown up and knew her childhood was over. A year or two earlier she had been wont to defend herself pertly, hiding everything under a stream of chatter. Now she no longer answered back, but listened to what was said. She began to weigh her words and to speak more moderately. She longed for a boy friend, and began to find happiness within herself.

Her views on life were those of an adult. She did not complain of the difficult conditions of life in hiding, but even here sought the good, the beautiful. *My advice is: Go outside, to the fields, enjoy nature and the sunshine, go out and try to recapture happiness in yourself and in God. Think of all the beauty that's still left in and around you and be happy.!*

Pampered from birth, she became strong and mature in spirit. She knew exactly what she wanted, had her own opinions, felt herself to be independent — an unusual outlook for a child of her age whose feeling of security usually derives from having someone to lean on. She began to develop a sense of self criticism: *Now the trying part about me is that I criticize and scold myself far more than anyone else does. . . I often accuse myself to such an extent that I simply long for a word of comfort, for someone who could give me sound advice and also draw out some of my real self.* And indeed, he who can criticize himself and his actions, and be more or less objective in analysing his own deed, certainly shows evidence of maturity.

Anne's self knowledge embraced many aspects of her character. She knew that she had conflicting impulses: *I have, as it were, a dual personality. One half embodies my exuberant cheerfulness, making fun of everything; my high-spiritedness, and above all, the way I take everything lightly. . . This side is usually lying in wait and pushes away the other, which is much better, deeper and purer.* Here Anne shows herself to be a natural psychologist. She is thoroughly acquainted with both her positive and her negative qualities, and is not afraid to state them.

While in hiding, then, Anne underwent a fundamental personality change. She attained a swift and, to my mind, almost adult, emotional maturity. That change was the result of the unusual circumstances of her life. Social and living conditions, it is known, leave their mark on the character of a growing child, but many of the changes in Anne's character may also be attributed to the growing process itself.

Even as a child Anne appeared unusually gifted, highly intelligent, and quite perceptive. And under normal conditions she would probably have matured more rapidly than the average child. But the stress is, of course, to be laid on the extraordinary life she led, which had a great influence on her formative years.

Rivka Manella, 16 years old, Israel

The Diary in American Schools

Henri van Praag

The influence of the diary on education has been so tremendous that it demands a special study. In many countries, extracts from the diary are regularly read in class. As a French teacher in Marseille wrote to Otto Frank:

"I teach moral philosophy in a normal school. Each year I read Anne's letters to my adolescent pupils, and talk about the books and articles that have been written about her in order to arouse their conscience and move their hearts. For those who have not known war, the facts belong to the past, and, alas, memory of them soon fades. But my students react with keen interest to Anne's diary. This year they decided to write to you personally, and they were so determined to do so that I have written to Father Pire for your address.

In what does the educational value of the diary lie? We have already demonstrated how movingly it presents Anne's high ideals and her belief in the future as an example to coming generations.

When we consider reactions from the educational world we learn a few more specific things. Identification with Anne becomes possible because the reader of the diary feels a deep psychological kinship with her. It is often the case, too, that Anne arouses self-awareness in the reader, gives him the courage to be himself. Reading the diary often leads to new discussion with parents and teachers.

Very important, too, is its message that every person, no matter how humble, can play a part in making the world a better place.

When the Chinese sage, Meng-tse, was asked: "If all men are essentially the same, why are there great men and small men?" He answered, "Great men are men who follow their greater instincts, small men are men who follow their

Examples of the use of the diary in schools. Scheme made by a teacher.

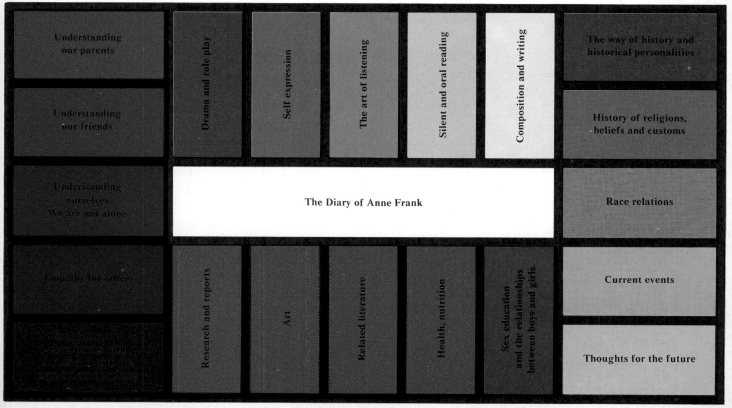

Understanding our parents	Drama and role play	Self expression	The art of listening	Silent and oral reading	Composition and writing	The way of history and historical personalities
Understanding our friends						History of religions, beliefs and customs
Understanding ourselves We are not alone	The Diary of Anne Frank					Race relations
Empathy for others	Research and reports	Art	Related literature	Health, nutrition	Sex education and the relationships between boys and girls	Current events
						Thoughts for the future

lesser instincts." The remarkable thing about Anne Frank was that she not only followed her greater instincts, but that she also had the gift of reaching others, so that they in turn were inspired to follow their greater instincts. And that goes for young people as well as older. A historian once said to me: "If I speak or write about Anne Frank, I always feel that I must give my best."

That is the abiding miracle of Anne Frank, that she has the power to move so many people to give of their best, and by doing so they confirm her faith in human goodness.

We find a fine example in an American school, where children of sometimes even the least privileged social class, because of the influence of the diary, have a constructive vision of the future and human fellowship.
Here are some examples of letters from American teachers and educators:

My work of teaching literature to teenage boys and girls and helping them to understand the complex problems of our world is a real challenge. Some of the great literary works of suffering and deprivation make a real impression on young minds. The impact of Anne's diary on my girls was tremendous, for they could easily see themselves and their own feelings in her writings. Her message of hope and courage had a very deep meaning for them. If we can help to make the hearts of men and women kinder, how great the world would be. Somehow we have not always listened to the messages of the past. And now the message of the present echoes the same to us, but some do not hear. Thank you for sharing your own sadness with us when you published Anne's diary. Her life will linger in our hearts, and perhaps influence our thinking enough to change the world.
Teacher, 1963

...When you wrote of the effect of Anne's diary, you may not have realized how universally moving her story is. I teach approximately 225 pupils each year in my reading classes. At first I was surprised that the boys as well as the girls found Anne's writing the most challenging of anything we read in literature classes. My pupils are usually around thirteen years of age, and while they identify with her, I think their response goes beyond that. Anne's story says so much about tolerance and good will that I have nothing to add.
Teacher, 1967

"WAR"
Child's drawing,
Miguel Flavio
Portugal

Each day our class reads Anne's diary, sometimes letter by letter, and sometimes selections from it which have special meaning in our lives. Even our slowest readers dig in as they want very much to share Anne's experience. I too find something new each time we read it.
Teacher, 1967

Last year, for the first time, I read your daughter's *Diary of a Young Girl* and was completely captivated by the charming, wholesome, and refreshing mind of that lovely girl.
I teach English at the junior high and the high school levels. I was so impressed with what Anne, as a teenager of another time had to say about growing up and the difficulties of maturing, that I ordered copies for my seventh and eighth grade students. I found that the girls particularly became as involved as I had in reading it. This year I helped to organize an extensive study of prejudice for our eleventh grade students, so that they might delve more deeply into this problem which seems always to be with us in one form or another. Your daughter's diary was recommended as a source book to prepare the students for our discussions. I find it so difficult to understand mass prejudice that I feel a sense of shame to think it could have existed, and does exist, and that it destroyed someone as fine as she.
Despite the terrors you have witnessed, please remember that there are people, many people, who abhor cruelty and feel ashamed to think that other human beings could be so obsessed as to forget the beauty and value of all life.
Teacher, 1968

As a recent English class assignment, I had my students write a letter to you. They have just finished reading your daughter's diary and I have read a follow-up article to them from a 1958 issue of Life magazine. My reason for assigning this letter was based on my conviction that a teacher, especially a teacher of English is responsible for instilling high moral values in her students.
This is a new generation, Mr. Frank, a generation which can only learn of the atrocities of the Second World War from books or by hearsay. Today, when prejudice, anti-Semitism in particular, is again appearing, it is important that every possible attempt be made to curb it. These eighth grade students are at just the right age to be influenced by your daughter's story.
Teacher, 1969

Poems written by school children on the theme "We Who Are Living"

We who are living
Have feelings
We cannot explain
We have fears . . .
We have joys. . .
We have feelings
Of love. . .
Of hate. . .
We who are living
Have certain duties
To carry out.
We carry God's love for others,
We carry our feelings
For others. . .
We love. . .
We hate. . .

Cindy Russell

To me war is a very awful thing
And it's not like swinging through the air
Feeling free as can be,
It's more like a jail and fighting
For your freedom and love.
We who are living go through life trying to love.
We who are living try to make life a better place to live
And we try to make friends with everyone
To show our love for them.
God gave us this life and we should try
To show Him we're glad He gave it to us
Instead of fighting.

Christine Latch

I am living in a world of war
Some people are rich,
Some people are poor
The people who are poor
Live in slums and in a ditch
Some are hungry
Don't ever get an apple core,
That is the world we live in. . .
WAR!

Kathy Mobley

We who are living
Try not to think of our fears,
We aren't always giving
To those who are our dears.
We try to think of things
That are beautiful and sweet.
The things that are of human beings.
And things that are of a great treat.

Though some do not care,
About God and brotherhood,
Which most of us try to share,
The thoughts that are good and understood.

Some of us like
To go to circuses and fairs,
To go on a hike,
Or ride a golden mare.

We have the deaf and the blind
The friends and the foes,
Some who are very mean and
Some who are very kind.
And others are unknowns.

Wendy Weigum

Our problems seem small and insignificant compared to hers and yet, we face many of the same everyday problems she had. We feel that Anne through her thoughts and writings has given us a clear understanding of how we, and people of our age, would feel and react in a similar situation. . .

"WHY"
Child's drawing
Herlander F. Ribeiro-Dafundo
Portugal

We are again studying *The Diary of a Young Girl,* and I think this year's group will get more from the diary than all the other classes. There is so terribly much missing in some of their lives, and Anne's feelings become a springboard for many discussions. I use the techniques of "role play" with this group — we act out our own feelings. Sometimes we read part of a letter, and the youngsters work out their response to it. Then we go on and finish the letter. The poem you wrote Anne (June 13, 1943) for her birthday has received much attention, and some of the young people report that this is the highlight of the diary so far.

We are going back to that poem in a few days, as I suspect it contains something important for these children.

This year we are working to help these young people gain some sense of themselves. I would like to aim our reading towards answering the question "Who am I?" and "What is my purpose as a human being?" Again the diary acts as a "mirror" of problems in common to young people. Never can I fully express my appreciation of Anne's diary.

Our class was lucky enough to be able to see the play again this year at one of the local high schools. We went not only for the content of the story, but also to observe some high school students who had the self-discipline to learn lines, to act, and to co-operate with one another. This was one more opportunity for our sixth graders to see what high school might mean for them. We had the opportunity of meeting the actors and actresses, and our class has more or less made pen pals with the lead girls.
Teacher, 1969

And from the same teacher in another letter:
The poems were written last week after we went back to your poem to Anne for her birthday. Then we read "We Who Were Born" as a follow-up poem. Finally the young people were allowed to express in poems whatever they wished. Some of the poems from last week were well done and others were not so well prepared. I thought you might enjoy reading these thoughts from this particular group of sixth graders. (Some used "blank" verse as rhyming words didn't always convey the thought they wished to express.)

Another group of papers includes the young peoples' interpretation of your poem. You really got us started on poetry this year. The interest in your poem dispelled the usual antagonism of the students toward poetry. For the first time they seem to feel that poetry can convey something important to them.

A third example we've included was the personal interpretation of some of the thoughts Anne expressed in her diary. The class was divided into groups and asked to decide what these mean to them as young people living in this age.

We are going very slowly through the diary as there is simply too much to be passed over lightly. We are not just using the diary for reading but as a guideline for finding meaning to our lives.

The people and thoughts expressed in the diary then lead to other studies which are still aimed at trying to find meaning. From the diary they are introduced to Churchill and Ghandi as well as Eisenhower and other prominent figures during World War II. They are also introduced to Jewish customs. (Right now we are reading the "Bronze Bow" which dates back to the time the Holy Lands were under Roman control and gives background for Jewish and Christian beliefs.) And then feelings and information are as fresh as this morning's newspaper of Mid-East turmoil. The fear of losing what has been so long struggled for by the Jewish people. The background partly being the exodus from Europe during the rise of Hitler. These are some examples of the way the diary becomes the center for many other studies. (Each year teachers often pick a theme to follow for the year.) Anne Frank and life's meaning is ours for this year. I include a sketch to show the way all these things become related into a meaningful education.

The History of the House on the Prinsengracht

Anna G. Steenmeijer

Amsterdam began to flourish as a trading center after 1585. This was due, in part, to the decline of trade in the Mediterranean and the increasing interest in the Atlantic seaboard, and to the sudden influx of refugees fleeing religious persecution, many of whom were Portuguese Jews who established luxury industries.

The merchants soon obtained goods from all over the world, more than they could sell at once, and the overstock was stored in warehouses. Amsterdam became the entrepot of Europe. The goods were shipped to the warehouses, which were built on the canals. Needless to say, canal sites were in great demand and deep, narrow buildings, consisting of a front house and a rear house connected by a passage through an inner courtyard, were constructed on the small waterfront lots.

Amsterdam grew from a city of 50,000 people in 1600 to around 200,000 in 1660. In a hundred years' time the city extended its boundaries four times. The Westermarkt was built in 1616, the Westerkerk from 1620-1631, and in 1638 the Westertoren was completed. In 1635, Dirk van Delft built the house at Prinsengracht 263 in the block of houses next to the Westerkerk. The house had both a front and a rear house. A hundred years later the house badly needed repair. The front house was given a new gable, the rear house (the annex) was demolished and replaced by a bigger building. Over the years it was used both as a private house and as a place of business by a number of firms. In November of 1940 it was rented by Dutch Opekta Company, which Anne called "Travis" in her diary, of which Mr. Frank was the manager. From 1950 to 1953, the houses on the corner of the Westermarkt and the Prinsengracht, together with number 263, were bought by the Berghaus Company, which planned to construct a large office building on the site. When the Berghaus plans were made public, concerned citizens as well as the Society Amstelodamum resolved to fight to save the house. By this time people from all over the world were coming to visit it.

In the meantime, Berghaus was having difficulties with its building plans, because the style of the new building was not in harmony with the surrounding area. In January, 1956, the company announced that another plan was being sought, and that the Annex would be spared. On May 3, 1957, the Anne Frank Foundation was established with the aim of preserving the Annex, restoring it, and opening it to the public; the Foundation would also work to fulfill the ideals that Anne Frank had expressed in her diary. Thereafter, the Berghaus Company presented Prinsengracht 263 to the Anne Frank Foundation.

Under the leadership of Mr. G. van Hall, mayor of Amsterdam, a fund-raising appeal for the Anne Frank Foundation was launched, with the purpose of buying the entire block of houses from the Berghaus Company. The Anne Frank Foundation would then allow the student association to build a student home on this block to keep its planned youth center near the Anne Frank House. The house on 265 was to be kept by the Foundation and made into a unit with the house on 263. The fund-raising was a great success, thanks to many private contributions, the German Federal Republic, and Mr. Frank himself. The architect Mr. Rapange restored the two houses.

On May 3, 1960, the Anne Frank House was officially opened, and the work of the Anne Frank Foundation began.

Visitors to the Anne Frank House in 1969

Argentina	1,087
Australia	2,650
Austria	725
Belgium	1,598
Bolivia	5
Brazil	916
Canada	5,228
Chili	232
China	74
Columbia	99
Czechoslovakia	147
Denmark	899
Dominican Republic	1
Egypt	7
England	8,538
Finland	204
France	5,343
Germany	7,852
Greece	256
Guatemala	2
Honduras	1
Hungary	91
Ireland	178
India	231
Indonesia	31
Israel	5,090
Italy	1,282
Japan	3,467
Korea	8
Lebanon	4
Luxemburg	28
Malasia	130
Mexico	523
Morocco	3
The Netherlands	16,651
New Zealand	742
Norway	379
Pakistan	31
Panama	1
Paraguay	3
Persia	12
Peru	28
Philippines	117
Poland	72
Portugal	103
Puerto Rico	67
Rhodesia	30
Rumania	3
Russia	246
Scotland	1
South Africa	1,205
Spain	978
Sudan	67
Sweden	1,951
Switzerland	826
Tanzania	1
Thailand	20
Tunisia	2
Turkey	92
Uganda	1
Uruguay	113
U.S.A.	97,775
Venezuela	138
Yugoslavia	47
Other Countries	446
Total	169,065

The Annex and its Visitors

They wrote in the visitors' book:

Oh God, why have the Jews suffered and been persecuted for centuries? They only believed in one God and it is no fault of theirs that people are evil. — U.S.A.

It wasn't done by savages — it was done by a people with two thousand years of "Christianity" and "civilization" behind them! It can happen again — unless we hand the story of Anne Frank to every generation. — Ireland

I hope that the world will understand our fight for liberty and freedom in Israel, the Holy Land. — Israel

All young people in the world should be obliged to read Anne Frank's diary in order to understand that they must build a new and different human society so that we may always live in peace, equality and mutual respect. — Mexico

From the story of Anne Frank we learn that the people who have power are easily made uncivilized and act cruelly towards those weaker than themselves, thereby forgetting that all people are created by God. — Indonesia

What we learn from this place is the importance of humanity. Humanity is the only religion in the world irrespective of nationality, cast, race or color. If we all can understand and realize its necessity, this world will be a much better place. Only with humanity will we attain universal decent moral and cultural standards. — India

We say much about peace and harmony among people irrespective of creed, color or race. But do we really believe and practice what we say? — Ghana

May there be peace among men, may God help us all to change. — France

I think the spirit of Anne Frank can do more to solve the problems of this world than arms and warfare. The work of the Anne Frank House is a step in the direction of peace, understanding, and unity. May God bless your work. — Ceylon

Anne, you are an example for us. There is still a part of the world under oppression. Let those who are oppressed not give up their hope and belief in freedom. Let us make this hope for freedom greater, each one of us in his own way. — Netherlands

Don't pray for peace. . . work for it! — U.S.A.

There is no way to Peace. Peace is the Way. — U.S.A.

I fear that the story of Anne Frank will be told again and again. One day perhaps all people, young and old, will come to realize that international justice is more important than national ambitions and war, no matter for what cause, and declare war a crime against all people. Until that day, we can only grieve for all the Anne Franks, past, present and to come. — Germany

The Anne Frank Foundation and the International Youth Center

Henri van Praag

The Anne Frank Foundation has set itself a two-fold task:
First, to ensure that the "Annex" is preserved for the future as a symbol of the past and as a perpetual reminder of the extremes to which hatred and discrimination against people with other ideas and beliefs can lead; and second, to promote creative meetings between people, especially young people, all over the world, irrespective of race, creed, social background and education.

It was Otto Frank, in particular, who insisted from the beginning that the Annex should not be a war museum or a shrine, but a meeting center for young people of all nations, and a place at which the post-war generation could seek ways to work for peace. Since the houses on Prinsengracht 263 and 265 were opened to the public on May 3, 1960, the Anne Frank Foundation has worked hard to realize its two-fold task. The number of visitors to the Annex has increased every year, to about 170,000 by 1969.

Each year the Anne Frank Foundation organizes meetings and conferences, at which problems of discrimination, democracy, cross-cultural communication, religion, and international cooperation are discussed.

The starting point of the whole venture was and remains the diary and the reactions to it. The reasons for using the diary in this way are closely linked to its pedagogical value, which is discussed in detail elsewhere in this book. Anne Frank had an extraordinary ability to bring out the best in other people. By choosing the diary as the inspiration for all the activities of the Anne Frank Foundation, we hope to influence young people, so that the future citizens of the world will be people who act on their best inspirations.

In planning the International Youth Center of the Anne Frank Foundation, we have attempted to link discussions to a visit to the Annex. Of course, such a visit can only be really worthwhile if the visitor has read the diary. The discussion periods often follow the visit to the Annex, and many visitors leave the building resolved to carry on at home the battle against intolerance, discrimination and fanaticism. Many Anne Frank Groups have been formed as a result of these meetings.

In addition to viewing the hiding place, one can visit the documentation section. This consists of three parts:

1. Documentation on the origin of national socialism and the occupation of the Netherlands.
2. Material on discrimination, intolerance and an examination of the roads toward peace.
3. Information on the work of the Anne Frank Foundation and the International Youth Center.

The guides, who are young students and members of the staff are always willing to discuss the work and the background of the Anne Frank Foundation and the Youth Center.

Our future plans include the establishment of a specialized library to contain material on reciprocal agreements, international cooperation, the struggle against discrimination and dogmatism, and the history of World War II and the occupation. A continuing program of meetings and discussions will help users of the library to find practical ways of applying their knowledge in the cause of peace.

Anti-Semitism and discrimination against Negroes are ever-recurring topics in discussions and conferences, but war and peace, aid to underdeveloped countries, permanent education, student revolt, and conflicts between East and West also receive the attention of the Anne Frank Foundation.

The Foundation sends delegates to international conferences, but most often the conferences are held in the Anne Frank House itself. Besides conferences and congresses, study courses and lectures are held throughout the year.

The Anne Frank Foundation also hopes to form an Anne Frank Association which will set up affiliated groups throughout the world, to pursue together the goals of the Foundation.

As an initial step toward this end, the Foundation has embarked on a program of cooperation with such organizations as UNESCO, the European Foundation for Culture, the Ford Foundation, the Father Pire Foundation, and the Sonneberg Foundation.

Eventually, an Anne Frank Academy for the leaders of courses and conferences will concern itself with the problems of achieving world peace. The question and problems raised in past discussions which dealt with freedom, democracy, justice, and peace will provide basic material on which to build the program of the Anne Frank Academy.

Some of the more interesting questions and answers that have come out of discussions at the Anne Frank House appear below.

Peace

Why do we talk so much about peace?
Because mankind wants and needs peace.

Why is it then that there is no peace in the world?
Because it is not enough to *want* peace, we must work for it.

What do we mean by peace?
Peace is more than just the absence of war or disturbance. In a positive sense, peace is *social* and *inner balance.*

Is this balance self-sufficient or does it depend on some other quality?
There is a strong bond between peace and *justice.* Peace without justice is a false peace.

What is a deed toward peace?
Every act of justice is a deed toward peace. "Peaceful co-existence" is an illusion, without justice. It can only be a step toward real peace, which cannot be achieved without justice.

Can unilateral disarmament forward the cause of peace?
Only if this disarmament is motivated not by fear of the battle but by respect for life.

Can a war ever be benficial to peace?
Yes, if it is waged in the cause of justice, as was the war against Hitler.

How can we promote bilateral disarmament?
By voluntarily waiving our authority in other territories.

Other important questions about peace included:
Does Russia want war?
Does America want war?
Does China want war?
Could the neutral countries of Africa and Asia help to promote peace?
Is Israel a stimulus for peace or does it merely provoke war?
What is the connection between inner peace and world peace?

Justice

How have we come by our idea of justice?
Our idea of justice comes from the Bible.
The Greeks and the Romans were familiar with the concept of individual justice, but it was evident neither in their culture nor in their religions.
Socrates and Plato, who saw Good as the highest Ideal, were exceptions.
In Israel the whole life was filled with the idea of justice, because the Lord was venerated as the Just One.

What is the relationship between law and justice?
Our law is mainly of Roman origin.
The aim of law is the *orderly* society, and the aim of justice is the *righteous society.*
By adapting the law to the demands of justice, we attempt to create a humane society.
Roman law aimed to maintain the *status quo,* while Biblical law stressed the importance of justice and righteous behavior.
This is a dynamic idea, that expresses the longing for a new world ("blessed are those who hunger and thirst for righteousness.")

Democracy

Are there different kinds of democracy?

Yes, in this sense, that the emphasis can be placed in various areas of freedom (for example: social, religious, political, economic democracy).

No, in the sense that democracy is always the form through which human beings always achieve freedom.

In other words, complete democracy is as freedom and justice a desire, but each historical form of democracy is only recognizable as such in so far as it tends toward a total democracy, does not in principle accept a lack of freedom, and in so far as it rejoices in freedom elsewhere.

What are the most important rights enjoyed by the citizens of a democracy?
The right of a minority to become a majority,
freedom of conscience,
the right of assembly,
freedom of the press,
freedom of communication,
and freedom of movement.

Freedom

What must we understand by freedom?
Wrong is the assumption that the free man can do everything which he desires. A good definition is given by Rousseau: "The truly free man can achieve what he wants and wants what he can achieve."

Are there different kinds of freedom?
No, there are many degrees of freedom, but there is only *one* freedom. It is inevitable that people in society give up some individual freedom for the sake of the society. The goal of democracy is maximum social freedom.

What do we mean by social freedom?
Social freedom implies freedom from fear, poverty, war, and hunger, as well as freedom of conscience, belief, movement and speech for all people.

How may the individual work for social freedom?
The individual must work toward the liberation of all mankind. Not one man will ever be completely free while another lives in slavery. Social freedom can only be achieved by the liberation of the world from the blindness of discrimination and intolerance.

The task of the Anne Frank Foundation is to work toward the goal of social freedom. We will continue, through international agreements, to promote study conferences and congresses in various countries in order to give the concerned public the opportunity to work with others toward peace, freedom, and justice for all. We hope that this will carry the spirit of Anne Frank's diary to the far corners of the world, and help to create the world of brotherhood and justice of which she dreamed.

Facts and Figures

The name of Anne Frank has been given to...

Schools			
	Brazil	Rio de Janeiro	
	Colombia	Medellin	School for Girls
	France	Menton	Anne Frank School Group
		Merignac	
	Hungary	Budapest	Anne Frank High School of the Jewish Community
	Italy	Pontelungo (Pistoria)	High School
	The Netherlands	Amsterdam	Sixth Montessori School, the school that Anne Frank attended
		Assen	
		Bunnik	
		Dordrecht	
		Drunen	Catholic School for Domestic Science
		Goes	
		Gorichem	
		Gouda	
		The Hague	
		Nieuwkoop	Catholic School for Domestic Science
		Papendrecht	
		Utrecht	
		Weert	
		Zevenaar	
		Zutphen	Nursery School
	East Germany	Halberstadt	High School
		Reichenbach	
		Tessin/Rostock	High School
	West Germany	Berlin	
		Düsseldorf	
		Essen-Bedingrode	
		Frankfurt am Main-Eschersheim	
		Hanau am Main	
		Hannover-Stöcken	
		Ludwigshaven am Rhein	
		Mainz	
		München-Pasing	The schools that are not otherwise specified are all elementary schools.
		Offenbach	

Homes for Children		
	Israel	In kibbutzim and children's villages:
		Alonai Yitzhak
		Bersheba
		Kfar Hanoar Hadati
		Kfar Szold
		Matzuba
		Neod Mordechai
		Neurim
		Nitzanim
		Ramat Hadassah Szold
		Sassa
		Sede Nehemia
		Share Avraham
	East Germany	Wismar bei Rostock (nursery)

Homes for Young People		
	Israel	Youth hostel at Tel Hai
	East Germany	Dresden
	Austria	Graz (under construction)
	West Germany	Berlin-Wilmersdorf
		Gross-Gerau
		Kassel-Rothenditmold
		Ulm

	Israel	Rehovot	Anne Frank Bnot-Brith Lodge
	East Germany	Bad Doberan	Anne Frank Pioneer Group

Flowers

A rose, "Souvenir d'Anne Frank," was cultivated by Hipp, Delforge and Sons in Belgium; and an "Anne Frank" tulip by Van Eden Brothers in The Netherlands.

The Anne Frank Forest is an area of 10,000 trees in the Forest of the Martyrs on the hills of Judea in Israel.

A few artistic reactions not mentioned elsewhere in this book:

Television adaption, by Walter Susskind, 1968, U.S.A.
Television program, "The Legacy of Anne Frank," by N.B.C. in the U.S.A. in cooperation with the Jewish Theological Seminary of New York. This program received the Ohio State Award in 1969.
Bust by Irmgard Biernath, Mainz, West Germany.
Bust by Gerhard Geyer, Moritzburg Museum, Halle, East Germany.
Anne Frank pillar made by Gerhard Rommel for the Anne Frank School in East Germany.
Portrait by Harald Hakenbeck, Dresden, East Germany.
Lithography by Marc Chagall for a French luxury edition of the Diary.

Documentation on Anne Frank is found in:

Amsterdam	Anne Frank House, Prinsengracht 263-265
Bergen-Belsen	Gedenkstatte
Jerusalem	Yad Washam, Har Hazikaron
London	Wiener Library
Paris	Centre de Documentation Juive

Of the publications on Anne Frank, the following must be mentioned:

Robert M. W. Kempner, "Edith Stein und Anne Frank. Zwei von Hunderttausend." A revelation of nazi war crimes in Holland at the trial of Munich. Verlag Herder KG. Freiburg im Breisgau, 1968.

Ernst Schnabel, 'Anne Frank, A Portrait in Courage', Harcourt, Brace and World, New York 1958.

Dr. M. Tramer, "Spiritual Maturity: Intellectual Ripening of a Young Girl with Literary Talent Under Conditions of Permanent Stress." Zeitschrift fur Psychiatrie, January-March volume, 1951, Bern.

The first edition of *The Diary of a Young Girl* was published by Contact, a publishing firm in Amsterdam, in June, 1947, under the title *Het Achterhuis* (The Annex).
The languages in which the diary has been published are given below, in alphabetical order, along with the countries in which it has been published.

Arabic	Israel
Armenian	Soviet Union
Bengali	India
Catalan	Spain
Chinese	Taiwan
Czech	Czechoslovakia
Danish	Denmark, Greenland
Dutch	The Netherlands
English	Great Britain, U.S.A.
Esperanto	The Netherlands
Estonian	Soviet Union
Finnish	Finland
French	France
Georgian	Soviet Union
German	East Germany
	West Germany
	Switzerland
Greek	Greece
Hebrew	Israel
Hungarian	Hungary
Icelandic	Iceland
Italian	Italy
Japanese	Japan
Kazakhstan	Soviet Union
Korean	South Korea
Lithuanian	Soviet Union
Macedonian	Yugoslavia
Norwegian	Norway
Perisan	Iran
Polish	Poland
Portuguese	Brazil
	Portugal
Rumanian	Rumania
Russian	Soviet Union
Servian	Yugoslavia
Slovenian	Czechoslovakia
	Yugoslavia
Spanish	Argentina
	Mexico
	Spain
	Uruguay
Swedish	Sweden
Thais	Thailand
Turkish	Turkey
Yiddish	Argentina
	Israel
	Poland
	Rumania

Acknowledgements

6. Memorial erected on November 7, 1965 by the International Committee of Neuengamme. It has the following inscription: "Your suffering, your struggle, and your death shall not have been in vain."

7. Photograph: Otto Frank.

9. Photograph: Anne, 1942.

10. Photograph: Party Meeting at Nuremberg, 1939.

11. Data for the chapter "Hitler's Bid for Power" have been taken from 'Das Dritte Reich und die Juden' by L. Poliakov and J. Wulf.

13. Photograph: A burning synagogue during 'Kristallnacht', a pogrom throughout Germany during the night of the ninth to the tenth of November 1938.

14. Photograph: Public humiliation of Jews, 1938.

15. The quotation from Mr. Koophuis is from 'Anne Frank A Portrait in Courage' by Ernst Schnabel, copyright Fischer-Bucherei, 1958.

16. Photograph: Facade of Prinsengracht 263 before it was restored in 1959.

17. Photographs: Before the restoration of 1959: the attic of the Annex, the workroom of the house, the Westertoren as seen from the attic window.

18. A part of the article 'The girl Who was Anne Frank' by Professor L. de Jong has been taken from the October 1957 number of 'The Best of Reader's Digest', with the permission of the publishers.

Photographs: Otto Frank, Edith Frank-Holländer, Margot (1942), Peter (1942), Mr. Dussel.

19. Photographs: Mrs. Van Daan, Mr. Van Daan, and Mr. Kraler, Miep, Elli, Mr. Koophuis.

20. The movable bookcase that hid the entrance to the Annex of the house. The photograph was taken before the restoration in 1959.

21. Photographs: The first diary with plaid covers and the continuations.

22. Quotation from the article "Anne Franks Selbstbeurteilung in graphologischer Sicht" by Dr. Erhard W. Friess, published in the 'Graphologisches Studienbuch' by Beatrice von Gossel (Frankfurt am Main: Dipa-Verlag, 1967), pp. 128-29.

23. Photograph, taken on Anne's tenth birthday, showing Anne, Sanne, Lies and Kitty.

A facsimile of Anne's handwriting.

Lecture by Dr. Mina Becker; details from 'Het Parool' of March 10, 1962.

24. Lithograph by Ernst Neizvestny, 'Anne Frank' (Russia, 1966). From Mr. Frank's private collection in Basel.

26. Article by Henri F. Pommer, republished in abridged form from 'Judaism, A Quarterly Journal of Jewish Life and Thought,' Vol. 9, No. 1 (Winter 1960).

Photographs: Anne, May 1935, December 1935.

27. Photograph: Anne, May 1936.

28. Photographs: Anne, May 1937, May 1938, May 1939.

29. Photographs: Anne, May 1940, May 1941.

31. Photograph: Anne, January 1941.

32. Photograph: Anne, May 1942.

33. Collage by Marc de Klijn, 1970. Illustration for the diary, May 3, 1944.

34. Mrs. Annie Romein-Verschoor, wife of Professor Jan Romein and herself a well-known Dutch historian, wrote the foreword for the Dutch edition of the diary (Contact, 1947). Quotation.

Mrs. Eleanor Roosevelt wrote the foreword to the American edition (Doubleday, 1952). It is reprinted here in its entirety.

Book jackets for the Dutch, American, British, German, and Israeli editions of the diary.

35. Daniel Rops, French historian and writer, wrote the foreword to the French edition (Calmann-Lévy, 1960). Quotation.

Albrecht Goes, well-known German writer, wrote the foreword to the German edition (Fischer Verlag, 1955). Quotation.

Book jackets for the Japanese, Argentine, French, Hungarian, and Yugoslavian editions of the diary.

36. Photograph: Mr. and Mrs. Frank, Mr. and Mrs. Hackett, Mr. Kanin, and Mr. Koophuis.

37. Photograph: The first theatrical performance in New York, October 5, 1955; Susan Strasberg, Joseph Schildkraut.

38. Scene from the motion picture, with Joseph Schildkraut, Gusti Huber, Milly Perkins, Diana Baker, Lou Jacobi, Shelley Winters, Richard Beymer, and Ed Wynn, 1959.

40. Photographs: The Dutch stage version. The play was staged by the Toneelgroep Theater during the 1956-57 season, and was directed by Karl Guttmann. The photographs show Rob de Vries, Martine Crefcoeur and Mia Goossen.

Bottom photograph: After the premiere in Amsterdam, November 27, 1956, Queen Juliana, Prince Bernhard, and Rob de Vries.

42. Johanna von Koczian played the role of Anne in Berlin BRD.

43. Photographs: Girls who have played Anne; left, Anna Maria Guarnieri; right, Milly Perkins, Mina Mitsui, Perlita Neilson, Milena Dapčević, and Ingrid Söderblom.

44. Photographs: Stage versions: Japan — Shin Kozo; Poland — Halina Piechowska and Adam Wolánczyk; France — Pascale Audret and Michel Etcheverry.

Quotations are from the play 'The Diary of Anne Frank' by Frances Goodrich and Albert Hackett, based upon the book 'Anne Frank: Diary of a Young Girl'. Copyright Albert Hackett, Frances Goodrich Hackett, and Otto Frank, 1954, 1956, 1958.

46. Photograph: Anne Frank Ballet by Adam Darius, performed in Sweden, 1962; television productions in the Netherlands and Italy, 1968.

47. Poem by Albrecht Goes translated from the German.

48. Statue of Anne Frank by Pieter d'Hont, 1959, St. Janskerkhof, Utrecht, The Netherlands.

49. Lithograph by Giuseppe Ajmone. A deluxe edition of Anne Frank, Tales from the House Behind' was published in Italy in 1962 by Cappelli of Bologna under the title of 'Il Saggio Mago'. A large number of Italian artists illustrated this work. The lithograph by Giuseppe Ajmone was done for the story "Rita".

50. On September 19, 1960, the Russian poet Yevgeni Yevtushenko published the poem "Babi Yar" in the 'Literaturnaya Gaseta' as an attack on anti-Semitism. The text was incorporated into Shostakovitch's 'Thirteenth Symphony'. In this poem Yevtushenko identifies himself with the Jews. BabiYar is a ravine outside Kiev, and it was near here, in 1941, that the Nazis carried out a mass murder of the Jewish population.

Translated into English by George Reavy, Caldz and Boyars. London. Copyright.

51. From 'Angel of Accidence', poems by Peter Kane Dufault (New York: The Macmillan Company. 1954), pp. 63-64.

52. From 'Zeit und Geist' (Darmstadt, 1960), author unknown. Translated from German.

53. From 'Tijd en Teken', a volume of poems by G. Boogaard (Nijkerk: Callenbach). Translated from the Dutch.

54. From Ernst Schnabel, 'Anne Frank: A Portrait in Courage' Harcourt, Brace and World. New York. (Copyright Fischer-Bücherei, 1958). Translations of the original German text were published in England, Finland, France, Greece, Italy, Japan, Yugoslavia, Norway, the United States and Sweden.

Head of Anne, done by Mrs. Betsie Sturm-van den Bergh, 1958, the Netherlands, and presented by her to Mr. Otto Frank. Anne Frank House, Amsterdam.

55. Photograph: Visit by Mr. and Mrs. Frank to Pope John XXIII in 1963.

56. Lithograph by Felice Casorati, "Kathy," from 'Il Saggio Mago'. See 51, above. This lithograph portrays a girl who feels that her mother and her classmates do not understand her. Behind the wall of misunderstanding, stand the children, who are laughing at her.

57. A letter from John F. Kennedy, and an entry in the visitors book by Golda Meir.

58. Rabbi Philipp S. Bernstein. The quotation is from an address delivered to the Annual Conference of the National Youth Aliyah Committee of Hadassah, New York City, 1958. A letter from Daniel L. Schorr, correspondent of 'The New York Times' in The Hague in 1952 to Howard Taubman, Music Editor of 'The New York Times' in New York.

Photographs: Compositions in memory of Anne Frank by L. Camberini and S. Chiereghin.

59. Photograph: Composition in memory of Anne Frank by Solomon Pimsleur.

Poem by Irene Oliver, "A Song from My Heart," Denmark.

61. Poem by Bertha Klug, set to music by her son Brian Klug, England.

62. Photograph: Anne Frank Village, Wuppertal.

63. Photographs: Père Pire in his study. Laying the first stone of Anne Frank Village in Wuppertal by Père Pire and Otto Frank.

64. In 1960, the Dutch Publisher Contact published a volume of stories by Anne Frank under the title of 'Verhalen rondom het Achterhuis' (American edition: 'Anne Frank Tales from the House Behind', E. Bantom Pathfinders edition. New York, Toronto, London), eight of which had already been published by Contact in 1949 in the volume 'Weet je nog?' Translations were published in Argentina, Denmark, West Germany, England, France, Italy, Norway, Portugal, the United States and Sweden. The stories published here have not been published before.

Photograph: Anne's room.

65. View from the Annex.

67. Photograph: Anne, 1941.

68. Facsimile.

69. Photograph: Anne, 1941.

71. Photograph: Japanese teacher and his students.

73. Symbolic portrait by Ruth Hartmann, 1959, Canada. Anne Frank House, Amsterdam.

75. "To Anne Frank," a poem by Gisela Merwes, West Berlin, sent to Mr. Frank in 1956.

76. Head of Anne by Mrs. Rosa Freeman, United States. Presented to the Anne Frank Stichting, Amsterdam.

77. Anne Frank Medal by Georges Simon, 1964. One is in the Musée Monitaire de l'Hôtel des Monnaies in Paris, and one is in the Anne Frank House in Amsterdam.

78. New Year's card by Gilbert Harris for the Congress of Racial Equality (CORE), New York.

79. Portuguese children's drawing by Pedro Morais, done for the story "Fear" by Anne Frank. In 1960, pupils in many schools in Portugal made drawings for a Portuguese edition of Anne Frank's stories entitled 'Anne Frank Contos' and published by Livros do Brasil. Lisbon. These drawings were exhibited in Lisbon and in the Anne Frank House in Amsterdam. Five drawings which have never been reproduced before have been included in this book.

80. Portuguese children's drawing by Maria de Campos Miranda, done for the story "Kathy". See 79.

89. Children's drawing by a pupil at the Anne Frank Grundschule in West Berlin.

90. Same as above.

92. Same as above.

94. Same as above.

96. Two Japanese dolls, presented to Mr. Frank by Japanese girls.

97. In the margin is the printed Japanese text of the essay.

98. Same as above.

99. Photograph: Photo Izis, taken from 'Israel' by André Malraux. (Lausanne: Claire Fontaine et La Guilde du Livre 1955).

100. Drawing with flomaster and ballpoint by Tamar Goldreich, one of the visitors to the Anne Frank House 1961.

Poem by the Lithuanian-Jewish poetess J. Weitschuneite from 'Magazine of Yiddish Culture', New York, Vol. 25, No 3 (March 1963). Translated from Yiddish.

101. Pen-and-ink drawing by the Israeli miniaturist Devi Tuszinsky, 1961, Anne Frank House, Amsterdam.

102. The essay by Rivka Manella is included in a volume of four essays: 'Four Interpretations of the Anne Frank Diary' translated from the Hebrew with a foreword by Mrs. M.L. Meelker- van Tijn, published by the Anne Frank Stichting.

103. Photograph: Bell in the Anne Frank home for children in Kibbutz Neurim, Israel.

104. Photograph: Menorah presented to the Anne Frank House by the Youth Aliyah on behalf of the youth of Israel.

105. Diagram for the use of the diary in the schools. Design Marc de Klijn.

106. Portuguese children's drawing. An allegory of the war by Miguel Flavio. See 79, above.

107. Four poems by American children.

108. Portuguese children's drawing. 'Perqué' (Why?) by Herlenader F. Ribeiro-Dafundo. See 79, above.

109. Portuguese children's drawing for the story "Fear," by José Antonio G. Pereira. See 79, above.

111. Photograph: Prinsengracht 263-265, 1969.

112. Photographs: Anne's room, the movable bookcase, 1969. Statistical report on the numbers of visitors, 1969.

113. Photographs: Visit to the Annex.

114. Photographs: Visitors to the Anne Frank House.

115. Same as above.

116. Photographs: Conferences in the Anne Frank House: a) Reception for the participants, b) The Chairman of the Anne Frank Stichting, Dr. Henri van Praag, opens a conference, c) Complete attention at a lecture on "The Rights of Man," d) Relaxing during a tour of the city.

117. e) One of the organizers giving information, f) Intermission between two lectures. Mr. Frank (in the background) attends every summer conference, g) A social evening, h) Making friends at an international party.

The photographs in the article "Hitler's Bid for Power" pp. 6, 10, 13, and 14 have been taken from 'La Déportation' (édition Le Patriot Résistant, Fédération Nationale des Déportés et Internes Résistants et Patriots, 1967). The photograph of Anne Frank Village in Wuppertal on p. 62 was made available by Hilfe für heimatlose Ausländer in Deutschland e. V. Aachen. Frits Gerritsen, Amsterdam, took the photograph on p 96. Bart Mulder, Baarn, took the photographs on pp. 49, 50, 52, 73, 76, 77, 111 and 112. Egbert van Zon, Amstelveen, took the photographs on pp. 113, 114, 115, 116, and 117. A. S.E.P. Textor, Utrecht, took the photograph on p. 48. All the other photographs and illustrations were made available by Mr. Otto Frank.

Text which appears on the endpapers was selected from the Anne Frank House guest book.

Ante el nazismo y el fascismo hay que
tenerlo un peligro latente. La vigilancia
debe ser permanente para ahogarlo al
nacer. Marisa Yáñez in
/ Uruguay

SAKSALAINEN VANHA MIES SANOI MINULLE: ÄLÄ
SEKOITA SINISILMÄISTÄ ROTUASI RUSKEISIIN SILMIIN.
TÄMÄ TAPAHTUI 1967 — MUTTA ME OLEMME UUSI
SUKUPOLVI, JOKA EI AJATTELE BIOLOGISESTI. MINÄ
SOLMIN AVIOLIITON JUUTALAISEN KANSSA, KOSKA
EN OLE LÖYTÄNYT SAMANLAISTA LÄMPÖÄ MISTÄÄN
MUUALTA — JA USKON ETTÄ ME ONNISTUMME.
MARSA, HELSINKI
+ INLAND

Impossible to express our feelings in words — a necessary shock which everyone
in the present affluence should be made to suffer. It is not something that is
past — wherever racialism exists it is happening still. Perhaps we can all help
to end this
Mr. & Mrs. Goldstein
Ontario, Canada

Dengan Anne Frank; kita
menemui KEDEWASAAN JANG BUAS
terhadap Kebotjahan jang murni !!
Roestam SINARO
Indonesia

Being an American Negro
I wish I could be as
understanding and
forgiving as Anne. She
is truely a wonderful
symbol to the Jewish
people.
Adline Boardman
N.Y
8-6-67